UNDERDOGS III:

LIFE IN THE OLD DOG YET

Gray Freeman

CONTENTS

ABOUT THE AUTHORS

Gray Freeman is a writer based in Manchester. He is a dog lover and enjoys walking and travelling.

Brendan Freedog is a former Bulgarian street dog, now based in Manchester. He doesn't much enjoy walking and positively hates travelling; he isn't that keen on dogs either.

Together they have written the *underdogs* series, which chronicles their human-canine adventures.

THE **underdogs** SERIES:

underdogs

underdogs II: DOG DAYS

underdogs III: LIFE IN THE OLD DOG YET

the underdog: a prequel to underdogs

ALSO AVAILABLE:

The Long Goodbye And Other Plays

INTRODUCTION:
BRENDAN'S BACKSTORY

Once upon a time, Brendan was a street dog in Bulgaria. He was caught, taken to a kill shelter, but rescued by a charity and brought to the UK. I met him at an animal sanctuary, where my partner and I were volunteering. Although I didn't want a dog, we had an instant rapport. I agreed to foster him for one night, but while my back was turned it became a permanent arrangement.

Brendan is approximately ten now; he has lived with me for five years, so half of his life. He is a mixture of different breeds. He's medium-sized, has long legs and a slim build, but a terrier-like face. He looks like he should probably wear a flat cap and perhaps drive a tractor. (To my knowledge he does neither on a regular basis.) He had a number of behavioural issues when we met and things were very difficult, but he's mellowed considerably.

I've compromised a lot because of my dog; I've had to. We're together 24 hours a day; we live together, we work together, we play together – though Brendan doesn't really play; he'd rather have a lie down.

I enjoy walking; he enjoys sitting down. I love going on holiday and exploring new places; he loves staying at home and not exploring new places. He likes seeing the same places every day - day in, day out. He enjoys seeing the same trees, lampposts, hedges, gates and gateposts every single day, and going up to them and weeing on them. And most of all, after a rigorous sit down at the local field, he loves coming home – the place that he loves most in the world. He loves stretching out on the sofa and watching daytime TV, or sprawling across the bed and having a nice nap. Brendan generally insists on sleeping for a bare minimum of 23 hours a day; ideally much, much longer.

Before lockdown, we travelled around the coast on a journey of discovery. Me, my dog, my van: it was a dream come true. Now – after three years without a van – we have a new set of wheels and want to try and recapture some of the spirit of adventure; we want to live that dream again.

ABOVE: Brendan in his travelling basket, which he loves – but only when on holiday. When it was at home he wouldn't give it the time of day.

PROLOGUE:
TRAVELS WITH AN OLDER DOG

After we'd journeyed around the coast of England and Wales, it was always my plan to go home and take a break and then travel around the coast of Scotland, thus completing my circumnavigation of Britain. I really wish we'd just gone straight ahead and done it. Though I don't know the area very well, what I've seen of the Scottish Highlands and islands I really liked and I know Brendan would as well: deserted beaches of white sand and an iridescent sea, that wilderness feeling and the freedom to stop your van anywhere and camp overnight. I think it sounds blissful. Brendan thinks it sounds less than blissful, but he would have enjoyed it really.

However, we had to come home because I had a longstanding hospital appointment for minor surgery. Then the van failed its MOT and was beyond repair, then Covid happened, we were in lockdown and there was no point looking for a replacement. Three years went by. Three years not exactly wasted, but Brendan got three years older in that time. So did I, come to think of it.

We got a new campervan eventually. Prices had quadrupled over the lockdown period. The new van was small and not a very suitable layout inside. Nevertheless, I started researching our Scotland trip and I was very excited about it. As you can probably imagine, Brendan did very little research and was considerably less excited.

We did a few local test trips in the new van to try and get to grips with it, during which Brendan seemed to be struggling. He wasn't happy with the van layout and he didn't like the colour scheme; he wasn't travelling well and he seemed very old and set in his ways. Furthermore, he's recently been diagnosed with chronic pancreatitis, an on-going condition that needs careful management and a special diet. If he became ill in Scotland, we could be a full day's drive from a vet, so – with a heavy heart – I shelved the project.

After a huge amount of deliberation and many screwed-up pieces of paper*, I decided we would do a tour of England's largest and most celebrated National Park, the Lake District. I have known the Lakes for most of my life, we go back a long way, we have a history, so it could be like a trip down Memory Lane. However, although it will be impossible not to recall those times, this trip isn't about nostalgia, it's about the present, it's about being here now with Brendan and enjoying the moment.

* Paper: the forerunner to a tablet/iPad. Some of us still like to use it for sentimental reasons or the sake of novelty. I save scrap paper for writing on, so as not to use any trees and further reduce my carbon footprint, though I admit I'm hoarding more scrap "writing paper" than I'm ever going to write on.

I'd like to walk up Lakeland fells and look down on a stunning vista of dales, rivers, the sea. Brendan would like to eavesdrop on people's conversations. I'd like to explore remote secret valleys and dark forests. He'd like to sit in cafes and chuckle at people's dress sense. I'd like to think that our trip will be a compromise, but I know we will be leaning more towards Brendan's choices. Anyway, these are the days that matter. We'll be living life and making memories. And probably sitting down a lot.

FACTS ABOUT THE
LAKE DISTRICT

The Lake District is a mountainous area in the Northwest of England. (The word "mountainous" makes Brendan very worried.)

It became a National Park in 1951.

It is England's largest National Park, covering an area of over 900 square miles. (This also makes Brendan quite concerned.)

In 2017 it was designated a UNESCO World Heritage site.

The largest settlements within the National Park are Keswick, Windermere, Ambleside and Bowness.

The Lake District is also known as "the Lakes" and "Lakeland".

The National Park is contained completely within the county of Cumbria.

The area contains 16 major lakes and many smaller tarns.

The National Park contains England's longest and largest lake, Windermere, which is 11 miles long.

The National Park contains England's highest mountain, Scafell Pike, at 978 metres. I have climbed this – Brendan hasn't. I would like to climb this again – Brendan wouldn't.

The National Park contains England's deepest lake, Wastwater, which is 97 metres deep, which is legally deeper than police divers are allowed to go.

The Lake District is famous for its band of poets, known collectively as "The Lake Poets", chiefly Wordsworth, Coleridge and Southey.

Wordsworth lived for many years at Grasmere. His most famous poem is "I wandered lonely as a cloud…" also known as "The Daffodils".

Stan Laurel – the Laurel half of world-famous comedy duo Laurel and Hardy – was born in Ulverston, Cumbria.

Beatrix Potter – artist and children's author – lived and worked in the Lake District. Probably her most famous creation is Peter Rabbit. (Brendan has never heard of Peter Rabbit, though we believe Peter Rabbit has heard of Brendan Freedog.)

ABOVE: Brendan sitting in front of England's highest peak.
He liked to sit here and laugh at the walkers heading up to
Scaffel Pike. I don't think he's ever been happier.

CHAPTER 1: BRENDAN ARRIVES IN THE LAKE DISTRICT

In which Brendan visits The Big One, Windermere, where he has a sit down amongst the crowds.

It's raining. It's raining really heavily. I lie in bed in the early morning, Brendan lies by my side, as usual. We're listening to the rain pummelling the window pane. Today we're supposed to go to the Lake District, which can be wet at the best of times – if it was less wet it would probably have fewer lakes and just be called "the District". I live in Manchester (Annual rainfall 364mm), so I'm no stranger to rain.* Brendan hates rain. He's from Bulgaria (Annual rainfall 670 mm) where he was a street dog. As the name suggests, he presumably spent a lot of his time on the streets... in the rain. Perhaps that's why he refuses to tolerate it now that he's a British subject.

* People always associate Manchester with a heavy rainfall, but this is actually a fallacy. Though it really does *seem* to rain here a lot, in fact Manchester doesn't make the top ten of wet cities in the UK and falls far behind Cardiff, Glasgow and Leeds, amongst many others. Meanwhile, London is way down the list in the 50s!

The short-range weather forecast is awful. The long-range weather forecast is awful. It just looks like it's going to rain forever, so postponing the expedition won't help. Besides, we're great explorers and adventurers; we can't allow the weather to dictate to us when and where we go.

But right at this moment, I'm struggling to generate any

enthusiasm for the trip. I'm a very logical person and looking at it scientifically – small van, miserable wet dog, lots of rain – it's not looking good. I consider asking Brendan his opinion, but I already know his answer; he would always choose to stay at home. But I don't ask him, because he doesn't allow any intrusion into his sleep until after nine o'clock, so the question would be very unwelcome.

I slither out of bed and head to the shower. Standing under the falling water I realise I'd better get used to this sensation.

* * * * * * * * * *

After all the stalling and prevaricating, we do go. By the time we're underway, the rain has stopped and the sun has come out. It's quite miraculous. It's like a completely different day. It's now at the other extreme and is actually too bright and almost too hot to travel. According to the forecast though, this is the very best day for weeks.

We head north along the M6 in our campervan. Our new van. We've been away in it briefly already – not very successfully – but this is our first big trip. We've not yet fully got to grips with it and we don't completely understand it's weird ways. I'm not impressed with it so far and Brendan absolutely hates it. I'm hoping we can put our differences aside and learn to get along.

Brendan really came round to accepting our last campervan and we travelled all over the country together. During lockdown it became like a summer house for him. He enjoyed just sitting in it and going to sleep. I loved that van; she was called Eagle One. By contrast, we haven't as yet named this one and don't feel inclined to.

We would never have parted with Eagle One, except that she failed her MOT and I was told she was structurally unsafe. We were three years without a van. They were dark years in so many ways. Campervans have since quadrupled in price. I eventually bought this one and paid far more than I wanted to, but I thought I needed it. Travelling is in my blood, whereas sitting down at home and watching daytime TV is in Brendan's blood.

The further north we travel, the sunnier and hotter it gets. It's roasting. We stop for a break at Forton services.* I slide open the side door to let Brendan out for a wee. After some coaxing, he jumps down and stands on the grass yawning. It seems the journey so far has been exhausting for him.

* Forton (now renamed Lancaster) is my favourite motorway services ever, because it has a groovy space-age tower. It opened in the mid-sixties, just before I was born. As a child I loved its space-city like design, it really appealed to me; it was like the future… but now! The tower once had a restaurant but it is now closed to the public due to current fire regulations, as there is no emergency exit. In the event of a fire, you'd be toast. Despite its redundancy, I'm pleased to report that the quirky tower became a Grade II listed building in 2012.

I buy a Costa coffee and two Greggs glazed doughnuts. You might think one is for my dog; you'd be wrong. I bought two because two are so much better than one. Twice as good, in fact. Besides, Brendan is not remotely food-orientated and he's on a special diet for his pancreatitis. I'd never heard of it before. I'd heard of the pancreas, of course; it's one of the inside bits, but I've no idea what it does, when it does it or how or why.*

Brendan has a wee, yawns again and then slinks off back to his basket, whilst I sit and eat my doughnuts. Both of them. I realise it was here that I stopped on the outward journey on my first roadtrip, several years ago, and before I'd met Brendan.* It was a different world then. It literally was a different world, pre-covid. But the biggest change for me was that I was a person without a dog and I had decided never to get a dog again. Probably at this time Brendan was on a roadtrip of his own, having been rescued from a Bulgarian kill shelter and driven across Europe in an adapted transit van to the UK. He would be rehomed several times, but would keep bouncing back to the sanctuary where he lived, due to his attitude problem and his obsession with Midsomer Murders.

* See the underdog

We continue along the M6 and suddenly there is a view of the fells. They look amazing: rock, bracken, rounded at this point, but still sturdy and imposing. I'm really quite excited to be on the doorstep of the Lakes and getting ever-nearer. Brendan is considerably less excited.

We leave the motorway and join the Windermere road,

which is winding and undulating. Brendan isn't very happy with this section. He's not really a happy traveller, not at the moment and certainly not in this van. I'm hoping he'll get back into the swing of things, as he once did.

We bypass the charming town of Kendal, home of the famous mint cake. Like many of the best things in life, Kendal Mint Cake was created by accident (like Guinness and Cornflakes) when a pan of sugar was allowed to overheat. Kendal Mint Cake is no stranger to Everest, as it accompanied Sir Edmund Hillary in the 'Fifties and Sir Chris Bonington in the 'Seventies. You don't have to be a Knight of the Realm to enjoy it, though it probably helps.

Just before Windermere town there is a fleeting view of the lake; it looks amazing, surrounded by trees, a glistening stretch of water, then it's lost again behind rooftops. The town has become quite a fashionable resort in recent years, full of stylish eateries and designer shops. It looks very nice, very attractive, but it's not for us – certainly not for Brendan, who isn't really a fan of people, even if they're wearing wrap-around sunglasses and Gucci slacks. I turn round to check on him, but he's nipped into a boutique and is trying on a pair of Dolce and Gabbana diamante-encrusted espadrilles.

Windermere merges seamlessly with Bowness, which is more seaside-like. * The traffic is virtually at a standstill because the drivers are kerb-crawling, looking for a parking space, but there aren't any. It's the last few days of the school holidays. I thought it would be considerably less busy, because all the families would be heading home and getting their uniforms out of mothballs, but apparently not. There are too many people, too many cars, too many dropped ice creams, too many squealing children, the tang of diesel fumes and the heat from a hundred idling engines. Tourism is now the Lakes' main industry – and by the look of it, it's doing incredibly well.

* Bowness – "the headland where the bull grazes" – is right on the lake. It's nearer to the lake than Windermere town is, which is quite confusing. To try and clarify the situation, the Victorians thoughtfully added "-on-Windermere" to Bowness, so its full title is Bowness-on-Windermere. I hope that clears up any misunderstanding. There will be a test later.

One of the very best things about the Lake District, is that you can rise above all this. Literally. You can set off along a footpath and leave the flaccid slapping of a thousand flip-flops behind, you can leave the masses to their chips and lager and doughnuts. In a very short space of time, you can be out on the open fells, climbing higher with every step, gaining height, getting a better view each second, breathing clean air, feeling the wind in your face. Unfortunately, with Brendan and his sedentary ways, we can't do that; we're stuck here with the holidaying legions.

I've booked a campsite in Bowness, a short walk from the lake. For me the idea of a campervan is to pull up in the middle of nowhere with a spectacular view and no one else for miles. For Brendan, the lack of reception and mains power would be intolerable. His idea of roughing it is a hotel with four stars instead of five. He will forego that extra star if the TV is large enough. If his hotel room didn't have a TV, he'd have the Samaritans on speed dial.

On the site, a nice chap shows us a few pitches that we can choose from. They're all a bit public and I don't think they'll be appropriate for Brendan. Then he turns and indicates a spot in a dank corner, slightly set apart from the others, shady and neglected. I'm sure there's heavenly music and a beam of light shining down on it. We've found our perfect pitch!

I pull the van into our secluded corner and begin our arrival routine. Brendan stays in his basket and has a rest after the exhausting journey, while I plug in the electric cable and make sure the fridge is working, so our tepid food can start getting cool again. I wind out the awning – this is a new thing – I've never had an awning before. It just provides a bit of shelter from the rain or – in this case – the sun. Then we're off. Brendan gives the site a quick once-over and wees on everything he comes into contact with, to prove that he's top dog, then we continue towards the lake.

The pavements are filled with strolling people and lots of dogs; Brendan growls at all the dogs – it's a full-time occupation. It's so busy. There are people everywhere and we're trapped in a throng of slow-moving pedestrians. Brendan doesn't like crowds – or individuals actually – but he's so much better than he used to be. He is on a short lead and walks along at my side. He will generally ignore people if they ignore him. It's quite frustrating though because he has to stop continually to sniff a tree, wall or lamppost, then wee on it. Or he will stop to listen-in on a conversation, looking from one person to the other as the chat goes back and forth. Often, he stands there with a shocked expression and his mouth hanging open, aghast. I've never known a dog do this before; he is captivated by gossip.

He suddenly races in front of me and stops, looking up at me. Brendan is a master of non-verbal communication and this means "Let's stop and have a sit down." We've literally just set off, so that isn't going to happen.

We pass a cemetery. A family is walking in front of us. The two young boys are on scooters. One surveys the headstones and breathily says to his brother: "Oh my god! How many dead people are there?"

The answer is "lots".

The brother points into the distance. "There's even more graves over there!"

Mum chimes in cheerfully: "D'you know what they do now? You put a QR code on the gravestone and it takes you to a video of the person."

"What… so you have to make a video before you die?"

Dad pipes up: "You can't very well make one after you die, can you!"

That seems to signal the end of the morbid excursion into mortality; the boys scooter ahead wailing and whooping, the inevitability of impending death completely forgotten. It seems to have made Brendan a bit depressed, but he stops to sniff a fascinating wet patch on a wall and then he feels fine again.

Ahead, I get a glimpse of the lake. I absolutely love water; I love boat travel. I could spend all day cruising up and down on the steamers. And, indeed, I have done in the past. We arrive at the pier head. The lake steamers sail in and sail out, graceful and elegant. The oldest is Tern, a Victorian steamboat, which wouldn't look out of place cruising along the Mississippi. You can't come to Windermere and not go on a lake cruise, it's impossible. Or nearly impossible, because we manage not to. We have quite a disagreement about it. Brendan hates boats, water and any form of transport really. Brendan and boats don't mix at all. Been there, seen it, done it, regretted it. He's completely inflexible and so we're not doing it. The list of things Brendan refuses to do is a long list.

Instead of a memorable trip on a historic steamboat, he decides he wants a sit down under a tree. I know this because he starts biting the backs of my legs. In non-verbal communication terms, this also means "Let's stop and have a sit down." This time I give in and we sit on the grass near the steamer pier. There are people everywhere, sitting on every bench, rock, pavement, eating ice creams, swigging from paper cups and cans, wearing shorts and T-shirts, sun hats, sunglasses, sandals. It's like the seaside in high season, though it's *not* the seaside and it's *not* high season - regardless of what the blinding sunshine and the impenetrable crowds might have you believe.

Despite how busy it is, the lake is beautiful. Windermere is the longest lake in England and Wales. It is eleven miles long (half the length of Loch Ness) and a mile wide: a ribbon lake. I've only just learned that it has its own version of the Loch Ness Monster, known as Bownessie, which has allegedly been spotted several times in recent years. It is supposedly the length of three cars – the makes and models of which are not specified. Not that makes and models would help me very much, as I only go off colours; Brendan is far more adept than I am when it comes to vehicle identification; he can spot a Ford Focus from two streets away.

I'm really not taken with the idea of a Nessie-type monster here. Windermere is over 66 metres deep, which might seem deep, but Loch Ness is over four times deeper (272 metres) and might possibly be deep enough to hide the mythical beast, but Windermere with all its boat traffic and all the tourists, surely not. I decide we should do some Bownessie-spotting; Brendan decides we shouldn't. For once I actually agree with him, so we don't.

The water is lapping, the sun is shining, the steamers chug in, people flood along the wooden piers, little motorboats phut-phut across the bay, yachts glide silently. Windermere always strikes me as being the most commercial lake and the most vibrant. It reminds me of the south of France – in a way. (Not that I've ever been myself.) It specifically makes me think of Roger Moore and Tony Curtis in *The Persuaders.* They often filmed them in the south of France and there was frequently a backdrop of water and yachts, sunshine and swimwear. Actually, Windermere probably isn't anything like the south of France, but it's almost definitely the closest we've got in the northwest of England. It seems quite cosmopolitan and exciting.

We have a wander about, but it is just so busy. I'd quite like a coffee, so we check out a glass-fronted café overlooking the water. Inside there is a queue of people waiting for seats. A woman in the queue turns round. "Oh what a lovely looking dog!" She leans forward to talk directly to Brendan. I tense. "Have you been for a long walk?"

Brendan just looks at her, completely disinterested. "Have you, hey, handsome boy?"

"Don't listen to what he says. We've hardly walked at all."

She stands up and looks at me accusingly. "He looks tired."

"He always looks tired. It's what he does. He's got it off to a fine art."

She nods and turns pointedly away. She thinks I've been overwalking my dog. The irony!

We abandon the café, partly because it's far too busy, but mainly because Brendan doesn't feel like a coffee anyway.

We head back to the pavement. It's difficult to walk anywhere because of the number of people; it's claustrophobic and quite stressful. I want to be up on the fells that surround us, looking down on all this. Brendan, however, wants to stay here – mainly because that's the easy option and will consume the least energy. As we shuffle along amongst the masses, he puts a paw on my foot, to stop me walking and to non-verbally communicate to me that we should stop and have a sit down. The moment we spot a patch of grass with no one sitting on it we lunge. We sit watching the people go by. At one time Brendan would have barked at everyone who passed, but now he listens intently to their conversations; I imagine it's in case he can get some dirt and blackmail them.

A lady stops and looks at The Boy, her head tilted to one side, her smile increasing every second. "Oh... he looks so wise, so thoughtful, so all-knowing."

"It's just an excuse to sit down."

She nods thoughtfully. "Maybe… but he still looks like he's thinking deep thoughts."

And maybe he is. Brendan is a very philosophical dog; it's possible that he puts so much energy into thinking that he has none left for anything else.

I too am guilty of overthinking things. I was a bit wary about coming back to the Lakes after an absence of many years, thinking I would find it a bit poignant, with many reminders of the past. And although it is filled with memories, so far the memories aren't sad. I'm here with my dog and that's all that matters right now.

My first holiday with Nicky was to the Lakes. We didn't have a car at the time, we were around the age of twenty. We caught the train to Windermere, where the line terminates. We walked for miles with our luggage, down to the clanking chain ferry which crosses the lake at the narrowest point. On the far shore we followed the lakeside path for several more miles to our bed and breakfast. It was quite exhausting. We had great weather: it was a proper summer and it seems very distant and quite unreal now, like a film or a scene from someone else's life.

More recently, probably a few years before I got Brendan, we stayed here in Bowness in a hotel overlooking the water. It was here – at Nicky's insistence – that I discovered gin and tonic. (I think other people might have discovered it before me, to be honest.) I don't remember much about the holiday – possibly due to the gin and tonic – just sitting in the hotel bar in the evening cradling a cut crystal glass, surrounded by dark wood, grandfather clocks, a huge fireplace and a crackling fire, with a view of the gathering darkness over Windermere. Happy memories from another time.

Sadly, I no longer drink and haven't for several years, due to alcohol causing migraines. Brendan also doesn't drink, though in his case I don't just mean alcohol, I mean anything. He has a phobia about drinking. And bowls. And most things. His favourite tipple is a muddy puddle – the more fetid and filthy the better. He usually won't drink any water at all, so has liquid added to his food to keep him hydrated. It's just another of his many quirks that set him apart from other "normal" dogs; he is very high maintenance.

I'm trying to help Brendan overcome his many, many socio-psychological hang-ups. We had a dog behaviouralist to see him at first. I tried to get in touch with him recently, but he is currently not working due to an accident. Instead, I read-up quite widely on the subject of canine psychology. The first thing to take on board, is that although we treat them like people, dogs are apparently *not* people: they're far better. I remember the psychologist, James, saying "Dogs always do something for a reason." So, you need to ascertain the reason before you can start to find a solution.

Brendan is a deep and complex individual, he's sensitive and has many layers – like an onion, which is perhaps why his lower half is onion-coloured. You can't ask him what his problems are, partly because if he actually answered it would take too long – as he has so many. All the psychology research led me to wonder what Brendan would be like if he was a human. Would he still have an eating disorder? Would he still wee on everything? Would he still be enthralled by *Homes Under The Hammer*? I spent too long thinking about it and decided in the end that it's maybe a blessing that Brendan is a dog.

I glance at him, lying in the grass, gazing into the middle distance – and I wonder if he's thinking the same thoughts as me. Whatever the case, we're suddenly jolted from our reveries as a jet fighter streaks across the sky. It's very low and very fast. Everyone looks up and follows the plane. The RAF use the Lake District for manoeuvres, to practise flying up the valleys and also for digital wargames.

Seconds later, the jet has gone and the sonic boom hits us, like an explosion, a tearing noise, like reality itself being torn apart. Then that also fades and there is the sound of birds and the steamers and traffic and the background hum of conversation. Brendan watches, but doesn't seem to be phased by it at all. This really is a step forward, because at home he's still frightened of the vacuum cleaner.

We sit for quite a long time; Brendan can't believe his luck. The boats come and go, the crowds pass by, on the stony beach the water birds waddle and squawk, and in the sky the gulls reel and shriek. A police van passes right behind us, with siren wailing and blue lights flashing. Again, Brendan reacts, watches it, but isn't unduly alarmed and doesn't raise himself from his supine pose.

Even here some crime is occurring. The chances are we will never know what it is. The police van disappears from view and the siren fades and that's that.

I gaze out over the water, chatting to my boy about my many memories of the area. When I glance around, he's lying down, fast asleep. They say your dog will listen to you non-judgmentally, but Brendan isn't a very good listener – evidently – and he's quite judgmental.

A woman wearing headphones passes-by, stepping lightly, almost swaying. She's singing unselfconsciously and has the voice of an angel. She is so uninhibited. Brendan opens his eyes suddenly and watches her, as though mesmerised. It's a beautiful moment. Of course, she might be off her face on crack cocaine, but we prefer to think she's high on life.

I eventually decide we need to move on. Brendan is less keen, but we've almost become a local feature and are about to be added to the town map. We wander back along the lakeside road towards the site as part of an ambling throng of people. At one point Brendan just stops and sits down on the pavement, causing a tail-back, some muttering and people having to step around him. This is his most unsubtle form of non-verbal communication, meaning "Let's stop and have a sit down. Right here." We definitely can't stop here, so I encourage him to continue with the flow.

Moments later, an ordeal ensues which brings the shopping crowds to a standstill. A small white car drives slowly past us and attempts to reverse into a recently vacated roadside parking bay. Brendan immediately goes off on one, jumping up and down, barking and snapping in a frenzy. The car has broken several of Brendan's rules. It is driving slowly: unacceptable. It is reversing into a parking space: unacceptable. It is a white car: unacceptable. It failed to indicate before blocking the road and attempting the manoeuvre: acceptable to Brendan, but unacceptable to me. People turn and stare, wondering what terrifying calamity has occurred to cause all the barking. After driving backwards and forwards on the same lock over a dozen times, the driver wisely elects to abandon and drives off.

Brendan is now on high alert and won't be silenced, barking a warning at every passing vehicle. I drag him away. They say you don't have a dog and bark yourself, but I find it really helpful. I take over barking at passing cars, which immediately has a calming effect on Brendan. As long as one of us is monitoring the deviant vehicles he seems happy and we arrive back at the site unscathed, but with me having a slightly sore throat.

A lot of people are sitting on deckchairs outside their vans, so I do the same. Brendan lounges in the grass; sitting down in a variety of places has really taken it out of him. I sit in my chair with a can of 0% Guinness. The can makes a most pleasing low crack when I open it; that sound is an audible cue to start relaxing. I pour it into a pint glass, creamy and frothing, watching it become black as it settles. It's so satisfying. I take a sip – a very large sip – and savour the deep, dark taste, smooth, slightly metallic – but metallic in a good way – a dark metal that's been matured in an oak barrel. Beautiful.

Considering how busy it is everywhere, and how hot it

is, this is by far the best option. I'm very focused on the present moment; the chair, the sunshine, the heat, the Guinness, my dog. Brendan strives to live in the moment. Unfortunately, it isn't as Zen as it sounds: the moment he's striving to live in is last Saturday when we were still at home.

Over the next couple of hours, Brendan seems to recharge his batteries and he's full of life again. It's still sunny and bright, but much cooler, so we head off for a walk along the lake in the other direction. We come to the chain ferry, which clanks across the lake at the narrowest part, saving a long drive round. I've been across it many times in the past, in cars, on my bike and on foot. There is a marina here with lines of moored yachts on the lake. I love looking at boats. I think boats are one of the few human creations that can actually enhance a landscape: sitting there bobbing on the water, promising adventure, travel, and sometimes seasickness and even drowning. I love boats, but – as I've mentioned – Brendan is considerably less enamoured.

We nearly lived on a boat. I seriously looked into buying a narrowboat as our permanent home. I did a lot of research into it, but in the end I aborted – because of Brendan. I think he would have grown to like most aspects of canal-living, but I don't think he would ever have got used to the noise of the locks, or the process of the boat rising and falling, or the proximity of other vessels and other people. So, regrettably I decided against it. But I'm drawn to water; I find it sometimes calming, sometimes dramatic. I love being near it.

Brendan's limited experiences of boats include the

Plymouth ferry. He made up his mind there and then that he was a landbound dog. He doesn't like swimming either. Or anything really that might result in him missing an episode of *Cash In The Attic.* We are so different. It would be easy to think we would be incompatible, as we don't share many interests; Brendan dislikes travel, I dislike daytime TV; I'm an insomniac, Brendan really, really isn't; Brendan seldom reads a book and I seldom wee at the field.

And yet, we are also very similar. I so often see myself in him; he is mindful, wilful, he has backache sometimes, he is often deep in thought. He is quite wary of people, he hates crowds. We both enjoy the outdoors; me for the views and for walking, Brendan for sitting down for very long periods of time. We're two sides of the same coin, whilst also being poles apart. We're similar, but not at all alike. We're more than the sum of our parts; we're two plus two making five. I'm not saying we make any sense – I really don't think we do – except perhaps to ourselves.

A family comes towards us along the narrow, fenced footpath. This could be problematic, as Brendan can feel threatened in confined spaces – and open spaces, and spaces in general. As long as the family walk past him there shouldn't be a problem. They do, until a little girl in their midst stops. "Excuse me," she says very politely, "But your dog's really cute." She doesn't make any attempt to stroke him, she turns and carries on walking. For Brendan this is a perfect encounter: a complement but no physical interaction whatsoever. Perfect. He trots on quite happily, probably wishing he had a cap so he could stick a feather in it.

As the evening wears on, the sun gets lower and the light is becoming golden. There are fewer people about, there are couples and individuals taking a walk, but no longer the crowds surging forward en masse.

An elderly couple come towards us along the water's edge. Without even thinking, I smile and say hello: it seems so natural; it's what you do when it's quiet and you encounter someone. "Hello. Nice evening."

Their reaction is very strange. They both stare at me, but they don't speak. At least, their mouths say nothing, but their eyes say: "Please don't kill us." They glare at me, then walk away. It's very odd.

As there are so few people about now, I let Brendan off his lead. He immediately gets lake-proximity madness and runs at full-pelt towards the water. Brendan running at all, ever, is quite an unusual sight, but to see him running towards water is really bizarre. It actually looks like he's going to run straight into the lake. At the last moment, he does a handbrake turn and veers sharply away, but keeps running about like a handsome dog possessed.

I'm a bit concerned that he'll get too carried away and just keep running, then realise he doesn't know where I am. He's too excited to listen to me; when he's like this he won't even hear me. I pull out my secret weapon; I sit down on a bench. Brendan sees me as he's flying past. He immediately changes tack and comes charging over with excitement. He loves sitting down alone, but a group sit down is just the best thing ever! He skids to a halt at my feet and lies down on the grass, tongue lolling out, panting rhythmically, gazing over the lake. We sit there enjoying the view, enjoying the warm air, enjoying being together. This is the first day of our trip and this is the best moment so far. It's everything we both want from travelling.

A man passes close by the bench. He is wearing a flat cap and Barbour jacket. He looks like he might own one of the boats; if he doesn't, he should consider getting one.

Again, without thinking, I nod and say hello. Without changing his pace, he looks at me. His face is set straight; there is no reaction. His mouth doesn't move, he doesn't utter a word, but his eyes say: "Why are you talking to me? I don't know you!"

He passes by and strides away. This is again very odd. Is there a pandemic of rudeness? This is very un-Lake District. But then I haven't been for so long, perhaps this is how people are now.

Brendan looks up as the air is filled with a sudden thrumming. An army helicopter comes into view, sweeping low over the water, travelling fast. The trees stir in its backdraft, and then it's gone. Like the ambulance earlier, we'll never know what it was doing or where it was going. Its sound fades and the lake becomes still. Brendan has barely reacted at all.

Across the water, I can see Belle Isle, privately owned, the largest of Windermere's eighteen islands and the only one inhabited. Through its fringe of trees, I can see the dome of Island House, its cunningly named palatial dwelling. I'd love to live on an island – preferably in a lighthouse. Islands are one of my obsessions; lighthouses are another. Brendan would love it as well, though he would miss his field and he would miss ignoring other dogs if there weren't any.

My first book – many years ago – was a cycle tour of the Lake District. It was a joy to research and to write. I used to come to the Lakes as often as possible, every few weeks if I could manage the time off. I worked in a bookshop at that point; I was responsible for the travel books and lovely maps. (I love relaxing in an evening with a good map!) I'd get the train from Manchester and then cycle all over the place, usually staying in the cheapest B&B I could find or I'd camp, regardless of the season. I cycled down lanes and trackways, byways and bridal paths. I really got to know the Lakes, not just the tourist areas, but the quiet places that are rarely disturbed by visitors.

It's very relaxing sitting here with Brendan as the evening descends. We both feel very much at peace. The air has gone grainy as it does as the light fades. There is the gentle lapping of the water, the rattling and grinding of the chain ferry and the chinking of the rigging of the moored yachts. A couple of boats tack silently across the lake and a solo canoeist paddles into the shimmering sunlight mirrored on the water. Everything is calm, tranquil, soporific even. It feels like the world is enjoying the last moment of the daylight before it's time to sleep.

There are signs of autumn everywhere. The trees are changing colour. The beech trees here are going yellow, the horse chestnuts are well on the way. There is often a nip in the air in the mornings. It's still August – just. We've had no summer as such, apart from the odd isolated day of sunshine. Despite it being sad to lose the summer, autumn is in many ways the best season. And autumn in the Lakes is stunning.

Brendan takes himself into the middle of the grassy area, so he has a clear view of everyone and everything. A group of young girls pass close by him. He keeps glancing over at me to make sure I'm there and available to protect him if necessary or serve him an aperitif if required. It helps that they're all female and younger and quite quiet. He doesn't bark or growl. He's wary and monitoring the situation. He's on edge, rather than frightened. He feels confident enough to stay lying down and doesn't get up into a defensive position. He will never completely lose his nervousness around people. As the girls walk away, I can see he physically relaxes and he suddenly looks anything but nervous. He gazes across the darkening water, sniffing the air, then flops onto his side and starts dozing.

I take the opportunity to Google Windermere. It is the largest lake in England. (I knew that.) Eleven miles long. (Yes, I knew that as well.) A mile at its widest. (Yes.) A ribbon lake. (Of course.) The current lake was formed after the last Glacial Maximum... (Well obviously.) Just before the start of the Windermere Interstadial. (That's exactly as I thought. It's nice to be proved right.) I slip my phone away.

This is the best part of the day for us. There are less people about and it's calm and still and very pleasant. This is the perfect way to enjoy the Lakes. I'm also very aware that this is a memory in the making. I learnt from travelling around the coast with Brendan that my fondest and most enduring memories weren't necessarily the ones I would have expected; they weren't momentous, dramatic moments, they were usually simple things, like sitting quietly on a clifftop with my arm around my dog. Sitting here now, I'm fairly certain, will be one of those moments that I will remember and treasure.

I always think the sunset is a very poignant time. The light is fading on another day and it seems to stir reflective feelings. As a species, no matter how much we're plugged into Netflix, Facebook, Zoom or Tinder, we're still inevitably bound by the Earth's rhythms and the coming of night makes us instinctively want to shelter in our cave with our family, huddled around a fire for warmth, comfort and security.

We wander slowly back towards our cave. Birds are gathering in the trees ready for nightfall – whole flocks of them. There is a frenzied chattering as they exchange gossip before bedtime. Brendan is listening intently, catching up on the latest news.

We pass a man with a beard and huge, bushy eyebrows. He's walking along with his hands behind his back, smoking a pipe, ruminating. I smile and say a cheery "Evening." He looks at me, chewing the stem of his pipe. His mouth says nothing, but his eyes say: "These eyebrows are heavy."

It gets darker as the sun sinks. I can't actually see the sunset, as it's been lost behind the trees, but it gets rapidly darker by the minute. On the lake road that was so busy in the afternoon, there is a steady exodus of cars. The car parks – that had vehicles queuing earlier – are almost empty.

By the time we're back at the site I've completely given up saying hello to people, which makes me feel guilty, because you shouldn't give up. So, I do a sudden U-turn and say hello to the next people we see: a couple from a neighbouring caravan who are returning from the toilet block. The look at me, as though in deep shock. Their mouths say nothing, but their eyes say: "I'm calling the police!" They scurry away – probably to make a call to the emergency services.

Brendan sits on the grass while I get the van into sleep mode. Getting the bed out is quite an ordeal and I can't do it when Brendan is inside, because there just isn't room for him. The main problem is manhandling the settee and pulling it out to form the bed; it's long-winded, awkward and tedious, and puts a strain on my lower back. Swearing at it certainly helps.

Brendan eyes me warily through the open door the whole time, because it's a noisy and unpredictable process. When the bed is in place, Brendan's basket occupies the last area of floorspace. At home he sleeps on the bed beside me, in the van the bed is too high and there isn't enough manoeuvring room for me to lift him up or for him to take a running jump. Neither of us like this; it's another black mark against this van. Another negative point is that with the bed out, most of the cupboards are now blocked and inaccessible. It's not a good design at all.

When it's all finally done it's getting darker and getting chilly. I step outside and beckon to Brendan. "Are you coming in then?"

He glances at me, but doesn't make a move. His mouth says nothing, but his eyes say: "I'm trying to distance myself from you; you keep talking to strangers."

I step back inside the van and he follows almost immediately. He hops gratefully into his basket. He's had a long and tiring day. Within minutes he's fast asleep. I get into bed, after all, there's nothing else to do once the bed's out. A crane fly is flapping around, repeatedly dive-bombing the ceiling lights near my head. I consider leaving it, but it will probably wake Brendan up, then there'll be chaos while he snaps at it. I catch it carefully and thrust it out of the window. Then there is another. I repeat the process, thrust it out of the window and slide the window shut. But there is yet another. They seem to be operating a one-in, one-out system. As soon as I've evicted one, another gains entry. Eventually I seem to have extricated them all and I try to settle down.

There is a whine from Brendan. He's obviously dreaming, because his legs begin to jerk and twitch; I don't know why that should be, because he's unlikely to be dreaming about running a marathon or even going for a short walk; he's almost certainly dreaming about sitting down or watching *Ready, Steady Cook.*

I fall asleep fairly quickly, but am awoken in the small hours by the sound of heavy rain on the roof.

* * * * * * * * * *

If Brendan Was A Human...

Human Brendan would be the sort of person who would sit in a café for hours, watching the life in the street, listening-in to people's conversations. He'd probably buy one coffee and make it last all day. And when the irritated staff came over and said rather starchily: "Is there anything else I can get for you, sir?" He'd say "Yes, a glass of water please. Tap water. From the tap. For free." This is how Canine Brendan likes to spend a morning, so I can't imagine Human Brendan would be any different. Except Canine Brendan – due to his drinking phobia – wouldn't be doing any drinking, and if the waitress put a coffee down for him or a bowl of water, he would back away from it warily.

* * * * * * * * *

ABOVE: Blue water, sunshine, trees and boats: beautiful, vibrant Windermere.

ABOVE: Brendan at Bowness, having a sit down and contemplating.

BELOW: Brendan is wondering why I've gate-crashed
his photograph and is not too pleased.

ABOVE: Brendan deep in thought. (He's trying to decide where to sit down.)

CHAPTER 2: SMALL IS BEAUTIFUL

In which Brendan visits and dips his paws in two smaller lakes: Elter Water and Esthwaite Water. He also does a generous amount of sitting down, before everything seriously nosedives.

I slept moderately well. For me, "moderately well" is really excellent! Unlike Brendan, who could sleep for England in the Olympics, I'm not very good at sleeping these days. I awoke early to the sound of thunder, a low rumbling growing ever-nearer. When the thunder came to within a few yards of the van, I realised I'd been fooled yet again.* I should have known because Brendan was still curled up asleep and wasn't reacting to it. He knows real thunder when he hears it and will react accordingly. He's terrified of it. It wasn't thunder at all; it was the first of the neighbours taking their sewage cartridges to the emptying point. Never having had on-board facilities (by choice!) I've never been part of the sewage circus, but it seems the earlier you take it the better; it's almost like a race to be first. I don't really understand it and I'm not sure I want to get to grips with the finer intricacies of the strange dance.

---

* Many things about this trip are echoing my previous van adventures. Although I must have stayed on campsites many times before, the first time I became aware of the weird daily sewage race was when I set off alone – before I'd met Brendan – to travel around the coast. And come to think of it, that was in Cumbria as well, at Silloth on the Solway Firth. (As featured in *the underdog*.)

I open the curtains. It's misty and dull. Brendan sighs and shifts his position; he doesn't appreciate early morning disturbances. He isn't overly keen on afternoon or evening disturbances either.

Over an hour later, the sun is coming out and Brendan is sitting outside on the grass, watching the neighbours heading to the toilet block with towels over their shoulders, and the last few stragglers striding purposefully to the emptying point, with their sewage cartridges trundling behind them, kicking themselves because they overslept and lost the sewage race. I don't know why they seem so disappointed, but they look like they're up sewage creek without a paddle.

Brendan is fascinated by all the comings and goings, so while he's occupied, I set about putting the bed away. It involves a complicated lift and simultaneous push movement. It's quite difficult, requires a lot of strength and agility and is the equivalent of an hour long workout at the gym. I'm guessing, as I've never been to a gym in my life. I'm not knocking gym-goers, it's just it's not for me. I prefer exercise that fits into everyday life, like buying cakes and then jogging home to eat them. Brendan is very similar, but without the food incentive. He likes to wander to the field, sit down for a very long time and then amble slowly home for a lie down. He isn't food motivated. He isn't ball or stick motivated either. In fact, he isn't really motivated at all.

By the time we're ready to set off it's a very pleasant morning. It's a winding journey along the main road which hugs the northern section of Windermere. There are tantalising glimpses through the trees, across the water to the wooded shores on the other side, but I'm mainly focussing on keeping on the road. We end up veering away from the lake and following one of its tributaries: the River Brathay. The road becomes more undulating and more winding and I feel sorry for Brendan, who's sitting in his basket, looking like a startled hen. The total journey is only quarter of an hour or so, but it feels so much longer. I know Brendan agrees. When we park up, he sits up in his basket expectantly.

There are two women parked in front of us, putting on big socks, heavy walking boots, fleeces, breathable waterproofs and gaiters; the only thing missing seems to be crampons. They look like they mean business. I opened the sliding door and Brendan jumps eagerly out of the van and does an elongated dog stretch.

"Hello." I say to the women. "Are you going far? You look like you mean business."

Curly Hair answers in a very business-like manner. "Only about three hours. Moving at a leisurely to moderate pace. Not far at all. How about you?"

"Not even three hours. Just to the café for a coffee."

Straight Hair looks at us curiously, but doesn't speak, but she seems incredulous and is smiling constantly.

Curly Hair nods. "We'll probably have a coffee first, then set to." There's something about her clipped tone and her efficiency and her huge array of equipment that makes me think of the military. Perhaps she's a dictator or something.

"Well, have a good day."

We walk away. Straight Hair turns and watches us leave, smiling. Curly Hair doesn't.

We walk around to the nearby café the slow way, with Brendan stopping, sniffing and weeing at every opportunity and eating a fair amount of grass. I could have imported a coffee from source in less time. When we finally arrive at the café, we've missed our early edge. The ladies are currently being served and a huge crowd of people have just joined the queue in front of us.

It's difficult being on your own with a dog – with a dog like Brendan anyway. Some people tie their dogs up outside whilst they're being served. This wouldn't work with Brendan. He'd panic and I'd be terrified that he'd get kidnaped because he's so handsome. He'd rather come in and stand at my feet. We join the queue. Brendan is very well-behaved, but it takes so long to get served that he starts to get agitated and probably thinks this is where we live now. The system in the café isn't good and the staff seem to waste an awful lot of time. It's also noisy, with a lot of shouting and various sharp clanging noises from the kitchen. It's making me on edge and by the time we're actually served we're both wishing we hadn't bothered. I just want to go.

It's too busy to sit inside, so we venture out onto the terrace overlooking the river. It's very nice, but a bit cool. I sit at a small table the maximum distance from anyone else. Brendan stretches out on the decking. The sound of the river is very relaxing, trickling over the stones as it wends its way towards Windermere. Fine shafts of sunlight cut through the thatch of leaves above. I take a sip of my americano. It isn't good. I have a bite of my Bakewell slice. Not great. I offer Brendan one of his sausage rolls. He sniffs it for a long time and then grudgingly takes it, as though he's doing me a favour. He puts it on the decking and then leaves it.

I'm starting to relax when an old man bumps into one of the huge square umbrellas that shade the seating area. As far as Brendan's concerned the whole sky seems to be falling in. The weighted umbrella rights itself, but Brendan flies off, dragging me with him. He won't settle down now, so we have to leave.

We head off for our walk, passing a hotel bar, The Talbot, where I've been with my schoolfriend Paul. We were wild camping in the area, which we did a lot in our youth. Pubs provided a warm refuge in the evenings, before the long hours of unimaginable cold and sleeplessness when you return to your tent. This was long before Brendan was born; probably even before his wayward mother and his absent father were born.

One night we returned to our wild encampment in some nearby woodland. I got into my tent and immediately crawled – fully clothed – into my sleeping bag. I could hear Paul pottering about outside and then I heard voices. I tensed. It was a gruff man; while you can't judge a person just from their voice, this character definitely and absolutely had the voice of a ruthless murderer. I tried to sit up, but realised if it was a roaming killer, by the time I had disentangled myself from my sleeping bag, Paul would be long dead… and besides it was so cold. Rather than making a futile heroic gesture, it seemed more logical for me to lie still and hope that after one murder, the killer would be sated.

It turned out that the killer was camping close by and in the afternoon Paul's tent had blown away and the killer had caught it and re-tethered it. (Don't tell him I told you, but Paul is terrible at putting up a tent and usually requires assistance, hence it blowing away.)

Of course, if that was now and I had my dog in my tent with me it would have been a different story. By which I mean, Brendan would have pushed me towards the tent flap, so I could investigate in case he was in danger. But also, if it was now, there would be no Paul to act as a buffer between us and the killer, as in recent years he has refused to sleep under canvas. And *we* wouldn't be there either, as I've upgraded to a campervan and Brendan wouldn't be seen dead in a tent anyway, so it's all academic.

Though we live quite far apart, we still meet up with Paul every year to go on holiday, so Brendan has met his Uncle Paul several times now and really likes him, by which I mean he will generally tolerate him, hopefully completely ignore him and only bark at him when absolutely necessary.

The last time we met up – we always meet in Wiltshire – was before I'd bought the new van, so I'd booked a self-catering cottage. I asked Paul if he'd like to stay in the cottage with us. He said he wasn't too sure because of Brendan and he'd think about it. He thought about it and promptly booked a room in a pub. In another town. Perhaps just as well; when Paul came to pick us up to go for a walk Brendan barked the place down and wouldn't let him enter the cottage. It could have been a long and difficult week.

I try to see through the window of the Talbot, into the bar area, but it's very dark inside. Brendan sighs impatiently. Apparently, I've been doing enough reminiscing and he's bored and keen to move on. We continue along a stony footpath leading upstream along the river Brathay, as it rushes through a wooded gorge. The path is popular and quite busy. I say hello repeatedly to people. No one is replying. They just stare at me and say nothing. Even the people with dogs aren't responding, which is very unusual. This was not how it was in the past.

Is this how things are now? Walkers have always acknowledged each other. Especially since I've had Brendan, people have come in droves to see him and reached out a hand to stroke him with an exclamation such as "Oh, what a gorgeous dog!" Of course, he isn't always. But today no one is even glancing at him, which is especially odd, because autumn is his season and the subtle changes in the trees emulate his gorgeous coat.

I say hello to a couple with a dog. Again, they stare but say nothing. But it's worse than simple rudeness, their looks are filled with hostility. It takes far more effort and energy to be rude than it does to say a simple hello. I don't understand it.

We bump into the two women we met earlier. This time Straight Hair speaks and she is enthusiastic and gleeful.

"We went in the café! I'm so glad you mentioned it! We had a coffee and a cake! It was absolutely gorgeous! We didn't know the café was there. I'm so glad we went! It's totally made my day!"

Ah, the uncontainable joy of someone who's had a cake and a coffee. My work here is done.

We bump into the two women at every gate. It's a linear path, so everyone is going the same way, but I still start to feel like I'm stalking them.

We – along with everyone else in the area – stop to look at Skelwith Force, which is basically a waterfall, where the river Brathay squeezes itself between a cleft in the rock. It's only a 16-foot drop, but the amount of water passing through is quite amazing. Brendan isn't remotely bothered by the roaring of the water and even deigns to have a brief paddle in the shallows, because he saw another dog doing it. We bump into the two women yet again. Curly Hair is less than enthusiastic.

"Hello again." I say.

"Yes… *again.*"

"Enjoy the rest of your walk."

"I'm so glad I had that cake!"

The main path is very busy with a snaking line of people. This footpath has a pub at one end and a café at the other, and great views, so it's very popular.

There is a queue to get through a small kissing gate.

We end up with the two women again. It's getting really embarrassing.

I smile awkwardly. "We must stop meeting like this."

Curly Hair doesn't smile. "Yes. We must!"

Straight Hair is still tripping. "I'm still on a cake high! I can't believe it."

"Well… Enjoy the rest of your walk."

"We're trying to!"

Once through the gate we veer off the path and sit by our second lake, Elter Water, allowing the two women to disappear into the distance with the crowds. Brendan sits down and enjoys the mild sunshine. He's either consumed by very deep philosophical thoughts, or he isn't troubled by thoughts at all; it's very difficult to tell.

The far half of the lake is private, only this side is accessible via the footpath, so Elter Water has a lot of secrets. It's tranquil, verdant, shy, reedy and mysterious… Despite the number of walkers passing by, it is quiet and unspoilt. I'm pleased to say this view hasn't changed even slightly in the fifty years that I've known it. It has a stunning setting, with the distinctive Langdale Pikes in the distance dominating the view and the valley.

I try to contemplate Elter Water. It's very different from Windermere with its boat traffic and tourism, which feels vibrant and cosmopolitan. There are no boats allowed here, only the serene swans grace the surface of the lake. I said that Windermere made me think of the south of

France, in which case Elter Water is… well, *not* the south of France. It's a calm, still lake, the home of wildlife, especially water birds, graceful swans and less graceful mallards. It makes me think it's the sort of place where Swan Lake should be set. It has a swanny feel to it.

While Brendan is relaxing – with his eyes shut – I take the opportunity to Google Elter Water. It is usually Elter Water for the lake and Elterwater for the village. It is the smallest of the sixteen official lakes and is getting smaller all the time, as it is gradually silting up. Though not obvious from ground-level, from the air it is apparent that it is an irregular shape and is actually three inter-linked small tarns. The name probably comes from the old Norse for "Swan Lake". I told you it was swanny! It is just over half a mile long and seven metres at the deepest point. Looking at it, I'm surprised it's that deep – but it's deep enough if you're drowning.

Brendan is sitting beside me enjoying the scenery… occasionally sniffing the air, occasionally spotting a dog over on the footpath and raising his eyes and his ears, though not interested enough to stand up and go and investigate. He's enjoying the moment, *I'm* enjoying the moment, the company and the view… it really doesn't get much better.

Looking around at the fells that cradle the lake, I've climbed every one of them over the years. I've walked the whole skyline in this area. Of course, there will be none of that on this trip, it's all about relaxing while Brendan has a sit down. He is desperately trying to teach me how to slow down and relax, but – true to form – he's not putting a lot of effort into it to be honest.

It would be a crime to not fall in with the populace and carry on strolling through this beautiful landscape to the pub in Elterwater village, have a pub lunch sitting outside the charming hostelry, warm in the sunshine, with the sound of birds and jet aircraft from all around. But the two women would almost certainly be there and there would be another awkward conversation.

"Oh… fancy meeting you here."

"Not much."

"I've ordered apple crumble and custard! I can't wait!"

"Well… Enjoy the rest of your walk. Lunch. Pudding. Day."

"We'll try to!"

I glance at Brendan; he's dragging now and has clearly had enough. We could probably get to the pub but we'd struggle getting back again, so we don't follow the masses and we don't have a pub lunch and we don't have an awkward conversation with the two women. Instead, we head back towards the van. At least I do. Brendan sits down. I carry on walking, assuming he'll follow, but he doesn't. He's sitting in long grass staring at me, but refusing to budge. I call him, I beckon enthusiastically and I call him again, with more force. He remains sitting and staring.

I'm not prepared to be messed around any longer. It's time to use the secret weapon again. I sit down in the grass. Brendan immediately flies towards me, running uphill without stopping. Within seconds he's sitting next to me, proving there's life in the old dog yet.

Once back at the van, we take a circuitous but very attractive route towards Hawkshead. Everywhere you look is a scene from a chocolate box or calendar. There are stunning views in all directions: dark forests, sunshine, rowans heavy with deep red berries, whitewashed cottages, craggy, bracken-covered fells. This part of the country is stunningly beautiful. It's almost *too* beautiful. Can anywhere actually *be* this picturesque without being computer-generated in a TV studio? That aside though, it's a terrible drive along narrow lanes with tight bends. Modern cars are too wide for these little roads and the drivers have no consideration whatsoever for on-coming traffic, or absolutely anything or anyone.

I need a break, because it turns out that being repeatedly run from the road is actually quite taxing, and my throat is dry and hoarse from all the swearing and pointless shouting at my opponents. Brendan also needs a break from travelling. So, I indicate and drive at a responsible speed into the car park at Hawkshead Hill: it's a hill and it's near Hawkshead. There are views over fells and forests. Tracks lead away through the conifers; the sun is shining and there is a solitary picnic table. This is perfect.

I pull into the only empty space, next to a motorbike, quite a flashy looking big bike. The helmet is over the handle bars. A pair of leather boots stand next to it, a leather jacket lies over the seat and huge gloves on the petrol tank. It's like the rider has disrobed and wandered off into the forest to die. I feel a bit uneasy and consider reporting it to the police. But I decide to give it some time.

Another car arrives and double parks. An older man and his two grown-up daughters step out. He's wearing a gold medallion, shorts that are too short, teeth that are unnaturally white and he has a sunbed tan. In fact, the only natural thing about him is his hair – and that's only because until recently it belonged to someone else.

He studies the bike. "Oh… that looks a bit ominous."

I nod gravely. "I thought that."

"Like he's gone off to commit suicide." He laughs and then they set off jogging into the forest.

I heat up my soup and then sit at the picnic table, with Brendan lying on the grass at my feet. I can tell he's concerned about the abandoned motorbike as well, because he hasn't immediately fallen asleep or asked when we can go home. While I eat my lunch, Brendan acts like security, intermittently trotting around inspecting all the vehicles and barking at any new cars that pull in.

It's amazing to be here, sitting out like this in the sunshine, with views that defy description.

I hear a rasping of tyres on limestone chippings. A man's voice, unseen: "There might be a picnic table if you want to stop for a rest and have a bite."

It's evidently a father and son. The son appears first, poured into Lycra, wearing a helmet. He's about fourteen. "Yeah, there is… But there's someone on it."

The father appears, red-faced and breathing very heavily.

He is a larger clone of the son, also wearing Lycra and helmet. They pull up in the car park and stand whispering.

I expect them to come over and share the bench with me. It wouldn't have been allowed with Brendan on the case, but they don't anyway. At one time people would have done. And it wouldn't have been awkward or uncomfortable, just a few minutes spent with strangers, talking about the walking, the cycling, the views, where they've been, where they're going, and inevitably the weather. Nothing existential, nothing life-changing – probably – but just a few pleasant words, like people used to do. But they don't show. I finish my soup and stand up. As I turn round, I see them loitering behind a van and I keep seeing their helmeted heads peering around at me. They hurriedly withdraw and disappear.

I head back to my van and expect them to take over the table, but they remain in their secret place, staring sullenly at anyone who passes by, then they mount their bikes and cycle off into the forest. Perhaps Brendan frightened them off, perhaps I did. I don't know. But they've gone. Good riddance.

A young man arrives from a forest trackway, wearing a rucksack. He approaches the motorbike and begins pulling on the boots. Evidently, the biker isn't dead. He's too far away to speak to and I'm lying on the grass cuddling my dog. He fires up the bike and races off, leaving a scent of cinders.

Like so many places in the Lakes, this area has many memories for me, especially of my last dog, Jake. To look at, he was like a black and white version of Brendan. I don't know anything of his history, other than that he was from Merseyside rather than Bulgaria. Unlike Brendan, he was astoundingly obedient; he never needed a lead and he stuck to my leg like glue.

We came camping here for a few days. It was late summer; the weather was fine and we were under canvas. It was cold at night and I was just sorting Jake's bed out. When I turned round, he was in my sleeping bag, curled up with his head on the pillow and he wouldn't budge. It was the only time he ever showed any rebellion, because he was very much a pack animal who knew his place. I was the pack leader and he was a follower and he liked it that way. Some dogs get a lot of security from knowing their role in the pack; they don't need to be the alpha-male, they just need to know their place in the hierarchy. Brendan is very much the alpha-male, which is why he flies at huge dogs that he feels threaten his authority.

That holiday with Jake is one of my strongest memories of him. Whenever I hear the song, *Seasons in the Sun*, by Terry Jacks or the Beach Boys, or even Nirvana, but not the boy band version, it takes me immediately back to that summer holiday with my Jakey.

* * * * * * * * * *

In the afternoon, we visit our next lake – we're really ticking the lakes off today – Esthwaite Water, one of Wordsworth's favourites. Brendan isn't interested in who liked it and who doesn't; he just wants to know if there's somewhere nice to have a sit down. I assure him there will be.

Esthwaite Water is small and verdant. It is more like Elter Water than Windermere, as it's shy and quiet, but unlike Elter Water it doesn't have a popular footpath running along one side. It is privately owned and a few years ago it received a lot of press interest when it was put up for sale on eBay. The asking price was around the £300,000 mark.

There is very little public access at all, so it feels unattainable and far-removed. One of the very few access points is a car park on the western shore which has a small shingle beach. We pull in, I pay at the machine and we sit on the beach looking over the water. At the head of the lake there is a backdrop of high fells, but the immediate surroundings are soft, rounded, green. Sunlight sparkles on the water, ducks glide past. It's all quite serene.

This area is very much Beatrix Potter country. She was a writer and illustrator, born in 1866 and educated by governesses and kept away from other children, which caused her to take a keen interest in the animals around her and nature in general. Being thus isolated also sharpened her imagination and creativity. Her family were from Manchester but holidayed in the Lake District at various places. As an adult she moved here permanently, marrying a solicitor from Hawkshead.

In 1902, her first book *The Tale Of Peter Rabbit* was published. She went on to publish 23 illustrated animal tales, often featuring local scenes, including Esthwaite Water, which is said to have inspired *The Tale of Mr Jeremy Fisher*, though the cover seems to show the frog rowing across Elter Water, with the Langdale Pikes in the background.

Beatrix Potter was also a merchandising pioneer. A year after publication, she issued a stuffed toy of Peter Rabbit. She had him patented, making him the first *ever* licenced fictional character. This makes me think of a brilliant marketing idea: Brendan Freedog stuffed toys, complete with realistic growl or snoring. Perhaps with moveable limbs, so he can be arranged into a variety of sitting or lying positions. I'll market it as an action figure. Perhaps an *in*action figure. Brendan is so excited at the prospect; he starts modelling one of the poses and promptly falls asleep.

A black car turns in and parks beside the van, occupied by a middle-aged couple. After a lengthy, unheard discussion, the man gets out and comes and stands on the beach. He says hello – so I'm highly delighted after the recent rudeness. Unfortunately, Brendan growls at him. The man sets off walking along the shore, towards a boat hire cabin. The wife remains in the car looking very glum and staring down at her phone. I don't at any point see her even glance at the view. A few minutes later I hear a whistle. The man is returning and joyfully waving two ice lollies at his wife. Magnums. Her sullen face suddenly breaks into a rapturous smile and she does a frenzied "thumbs up" gesture.

They eat their Magnums in the car, then the man gets out and has another walk about and takes a few photos of the view. The wife remains in the car, messing with her phone. When their parking ticket runs out, after an hour, they drive off, with the woman not once setting foot outside the car.

I sit on the beach drinking my van-brewed tea, my arm

around my dog. Solitary leaves flutter down around us. Brendan is so relaxed he's letting the ducks slide past without barking at them. I'm eating the remainder of my Bakewell tart from the morning. The ducks are getting ever closer; I think they want some of the cake. I'm afraid they aren't successful.

I look at the beautiful view and try to decide what I feel about Esthwaite Water. Clearly, Brendan loves it: we've only had to walk five yards from the van to the beach and we're having a sit down! This is definitely his sort of lake.

There is the sound of the wind in the rushes, like dried paper, and the flapping of birds' wings. A flotilla of mallards and a lone grebe swim past. Then two swans and their solitary cygnet. If I had to pick one word to describe Esthwaite Water, it would probably be "tranquil". Or "unknown". Or "private". Or "picturesque". I'm not very good at limiting my adjectives, but I think I'd stick with tranquil. If Brendan had to pick one word he would probably pick "Bonio". Not because the lake in any way resembles or has any connection with Bonios, but that's dogs for you.

Esthwaite Water is quite diverse in its mood and landscapes. Depending on where you are on its shoreline, some of the backdrops look really dark and foreboding, miles of impenetrable, brooding coniferous forest, whilst other parts are soft and green and rolling, with attractive cottages overlooking the water, yet other areas seem barren and empty. I like Esthwaite Water. I like its diversity, but I don't really feel I know it, though I think I know it as well as I can ever know this rather private lake.

We could both have stayed here looking at the view and absorbing the calm, but our parking ticket expires and we continue driving around the lake, to the charming village of Near Sawrey, where Beatrix Potter bought the 17th Century Hill Top farm. Although the house is rather plain and grey, the garden is colourful and very striking; both feature in many of her illustrations. She bequeathed Hill Top and much of her estate to the National Trust, as she had great affection for conservation. It would be a crime not to visit this historic property, but as I'm with Brendan I don't think any judge would find me guilty. We drive on, heading back towards Windermere.

It's a gruelling drive along very narrow, winding lanes. Again, I frequently pull in to let on-coming vehicles pass, but not one person says thank you or offers any acknowledgement. Not one.

The drive is arduous, but through absolutely stunning countryside, beneath overhanging trees, between high, flowering hedgerows. We pass beautiful Lakeland cottages built of local slate, surrounded by flowers, hanging baskets, window boxes. These are quaint, quiet, seldom-used byways. This is part of the secret Lake District, unknown, unspoilt.

We call very briefly into the National Trust's Wray Castle, a stunning early Victorian neo-gothic mock castle on the western shore of Windermere. It's an imposing, theatrical, almost Disneyesque creation of turrets and towers and battlements. This was one of the country houses where the young Beatrix Potter and her family spent their summers. The main reason for my visit is to look at the adjacent Dower House, which stands in the castle grounds. This was the B&B that Nicky and I came to on our first holiday. I'm pleased to see it's still a B&B. It's in a stunning location with views down over Windermere. Unfortunately, the car park is completely full and I can't stop – which is perhaps a blessing, as the parking charges are extortionate.

We continue back towards our campsite. The roads are so tight and yet again I get run into the hedge several times because of people in huge cars that they can't handle; they come careering round the corners on the wrong side. I find this journey very stressful and I've got a pain in my right-hand side, just below my ribs. I've had it on and off for a few days – I assumed it was IBS brought on by stress – but it's getting more severe and it's starting to make me wince. I'm very glad when we're back in our dank corner on the site and I can relax.

I text Nicky to see how her day in the office is going. The pain isn't subsiding now that I'm no longer driving, in fact, it's getting worse and is sharp and twisting, coming in waves and taking my breath away. I mention this to her and she phones immediately. She has a fine grasp of healthcare after years of dipping in and out of *Casualty* – the programme, not the place – and also binge-watching *ER,* and *St Elsewhere*, so she's virtually a doctor. Her concern is that it might be appendicitis, which – if ignored – can burst and kill you. This isn't how I wanted to spend this trip. I assure her it's not appendicitis, though the pain is so severe now that I keep thinking I'm either going to black out or vomit. I take some comfort from the fact that Brendan is relaxing on the grass and showing no concern whatsoever.

Nicky has found an NHS questionnaire online and begins asking me a series of questions. I seem to be getting most of them right, so I'm feeling quite smug, until there is another wave of pain and I feel considerably less smug. We finish the questionnaire and the result comes in.

There is concern in her voice. "It says phone your GP immediately."

I have a smothering, sinking feeling, but it's quickly quashed by the pain. "It's 4.58. There'll be no one there."

"You've got two minutes." she insists. "Phone them now!"

It's difficult to get through to the surgery at the best of times and 4.58 is never the best of times, except perhaps for the receptionists who are packing up ready to go home. Like everywhere now, you go into an automated queue. I was expecting "You are in a queue. You are at position... twenty-*six*." There's absolutely no chance. It's 4.59 and counting.

This is such a waste of time! Then the call connects! I steel myself. I hear the electronic voice: "You are in a queue. You are at position... *one*." I can't believe it! Of course, it doesn't mean anyone will actually take the call. I can see the receptionist pulling on her coat and switching off her computer. A second later a real humanoid person answers! It's caught me off guard and I now can't remember why I'm phoning. Right on cue, a wave of pain shoots through my upper right quadrant to remind me.

She listens to my problem and then says she'll get the on-call doctor to phone me back as soon as possible.

Which he does, very promptly. He's very friendly and very helpful. He says it may well not be appendicitis, but the pain is emanating from the correct area, so it would be unwise to do nothing. He gives me three options. I can go to an A&E department somewhere locally – the nearest being Barrow, nearly 30 miles away along winding roads; I can go home and go to my local A&E department – nearly 100 miles away; or I can go home and go to an emergency appointment with the GP tomorrow, assuming I survive the night and successfully complete the homeward journey. He underlines that doing nothing would be foolish.

I really don't know what to do. None of the options are acceptable. He makes the emergency appointment for tomorrow, saying I can always cancel it. If I feel worse, I should go to A&E immediately, if I get *considerably* worse – he gives me a list of symptoms including vomiting – I should call an ambulance. Apparently, you don't drop dead from appendicitis without fair warning, which is comforting. In a way. But not very much. I look out at Brendan, stretched out on the grass, still enjoying the sunshine, carefree and contented. He'll be gutted.

"It looks like we might have to cut our trip short, boy." I say. But before I've finished the sentence, he's in the van with his case packed, checking the road atlas and assuming his travel position.

I phone Nicky back and we discuss every option in detail. She offers to drive over, but that will take over two hours with the traffic and I don't want her driving all that way when she's tired and she'll be stressed. It would take an hour to get to the local A&E, and then I'd have to leave

Brendan alone in the van. I'm not doing that. And then if I got kept in what would happen? I consider leaving him in the van, here on the site and I ask the site staff to keep an eye on him – not do anything, just make sure the van is alright. They are quite unhelpful and refuse. I did underline the life-threatening aspect of a bursting appendix, but it was still a no.

I tell Nicky I'm thinking of doing nothing, as it's just stress, and I'll have an early night and I'm sure I'll feel fine in the morning. She isn't having any of this. "If your appendix bursts in the night you can die!" She's the one with the medical drama training, so she should know. She says if I don't do something she will be forced to drive over.

I hate it when there isn't a right answer, only a choice between wrong answers. I am very logical and methodical and I always consider everything very carefully before making a decision. And I'm at a stalemate. I don't know what to do, but my main concern is for Brendan. I don't believe this is appendicitis; my only reason for going along with the hospital route is to rule appendicitis out. Really, it's quite concerning that the options the on-call doctor gave me all involve me driving a long way on quite hazardous roads. If it *is* appendicitis, surely this couldn't be a good thing?

In the end, I unplug the electric cable, wind in the awning and drive off, whilst the neighbours saunter back from the restaurants and bars in the balmy evening.

By this stage, the pain has subsided. As I bomb along the motorway heading south, heading home, I feel fine and I don't want to abort my holiday. But I'm also aware that I do need to get this checked out, because some parts of the Lakes are remote valleys and if I was ill there it could be potentially very bad.

We drive back through the darkness. Despite roadworks we are home within 90 minutes and tucked up in our own bed. I'm gutted that our trip has come to an untimely end in less than 48 hours.

* * * * * * * * * *

If Brendan Was A Human...

Human Brendan won't be told what to do. He's an anarchist, he's a rebel, he's a maverick. If you tell him to turn right, he'll turn left. If you tell him to stop, he'll go. He isn't *trying* to be awkward; he doesn't *need* to try. He's just naturally contradictory.

ABOVE: Still Life: Esthwaite Water. And duck.

ABOVE: They say people still talk about it... the time Brendan stood up for no reason at all... and then stood still for a while. This photo proves it actually happened.

ABOVE: Normal service is restored: Brendan relaxes at Elter Water.

ABOVE: Sunshine, the countryside and my boy.

CHAPTER 3: GOING NOWHERE

In which we try to start the second leg of our trip. Does it go according to plan? Not even slightly. (Though there is a chance that it does go exactly to Brendan's plan.)

I had quite a lot of pain in the night and it kept me awake. Brendan, however, had no trouble sleeping. He was delighted to be back in his own bed. Now that the morning has finally come, I don't feel as well as I hoped I would. The pain isn't constant at present; it comes in spasms and is much less severe than it had been in the Lakes, but it's still quite sharp when it comes.

I open the curtains on a bright, sunny day and I wish it was raining. I feel absolutely gutted that our trip has skittered to a halt and the fine weather is just adding insult to injury.

At Brendan's insistence, we set off to the field – known locally as Brendan's Field. Many of the regulars come and we're greeted with a barrage of questions: "I thought you'd gone away." "Didn't you go away in the end?" "Are you back already?" People are very nice and very concerned when I relate what's happened.

Brendan sits on the low hill, known – not surprisingly – as Brendan's Hill. He's holding court, while his subjects – both human and canine – flock around him. At one point, Duggie and Louis seem to be chatting to him. I imagine the conversation goes along the lines of: "Hi, Brendan, I thought you'd gone away."

"Get off my field! It's members only!" It's Brendan's Field and he isn't a very good host.

It's actually quite hot and everyone moves into the shade of the trees on Brendan's Hill, apart from Brendan himself, who slinks off across the field to have a bit of "me time".

I bemoan how busy it was in the Lakes and say I hope when we return – probably at the weekend, the last days of the school holidays – it will hopefully be considerably less busy. I haven't yet had the awkward conversation with Brendan that yes, we're going back.

In the late morning, I leave Brendan alone at home – something I very rarely do – whilst I go to the doctors for my emergency appointment. I see a very attentive young doctor, who pokes and prods me. He says they will need to take some blood and run some tests and at some point, I'll have to have an ultrasound, but in all likelihood, it isn't my appendix. That's good! But possibly my pancreas. Probably not so good. Or my gall bladder. Also not so good? So, I leave a sample of blood – I seem to leave an awful lot there these days – and have to await an ultrasound appointment to be scheduled for me.

The doctor also suggested perhaps it was too much processed food, because I was living in my van. I eat very healthily at home, supplemented by cakes, and although I eat healthily in my van with lots of fruit, salad and so forth, there is a higher processed content. This is something I need to watch out for.

I'm always saying how similar I am to Brendan – then again, I'm always saying how *dis*similar we are – I suppose it depends on which day you catch me. It seems we're possibly afflicted with the same – or similar – ailment.

* * * * * * * * * *

It's a Saturday. A beautiful sunny day, but very hot. It's my intention to set off back to the Lakes today. It's Brendan's intention never to go back. I decide it's too hot to travel during the day; Brendan decides it's too hot to travel ever.

It really is unseasonably, freakishly hot and the van is like a furnace and quite airless, even with the windows open. It's considerably cooler in the back where Brendan sits with many of the curtains closed, compared to the cab, which is like being in a greenhouse; it's not generally acceptable to close the curtains when you're driving. We decide to travel at night, after dark. Brendan travels better in darkness and hopefully it will be cooler and less busy.

We get a Chinese takeaway with Nicky in the evening. Unfortunately, it's quite horrible. We say our goodbyes – for the second time in a matter of days – and we drive away at 9 o'clock. We head off into the darkness – like all great adventurers. Or at least those who leave at nighttime.

Brendan's had a very full-on day: relaxing, napping, occasionally strolling, a bit of sitting down and a few episodes of *Four In A Bed,* so he's more than ready for a serious sleep. He's curled up in his basket and seems very comfortable as we cruise through the cloying orange glow of the M60. There is very little traffic and all is well.

There is a huge, low tangerine moon. It's not quite full, but still basically round. It isn't the usual white moon, this is like a huge fiery ball in the sky. It's so vivid it looks false. Ancient tribes – or the villagers in *The Wicker Man* – would probably have been terrified and thought the gods were angry with them and they'd need to do a sacrifice. It certainly looks like a bad omen. And that's exactly what it is.

There are roadworks ahead and we're being funnelled between traffic cones away from the junction we need to join the M61. There are no options, I just have to continue ahead in the slow-moving line of traffic. I immediately start to feel stressed and anxious. I just want to get to the Lakes, park up somewhere and sleep until dawn and I know Brendan wants the same – but without the "going to the Lakes" part.

It seems ages to the next available junction, though that's probably a lot to do with the speed we're travelling. I turn off, go around a roundabout – at which point Brendan sits up in his basket curiously, in case we're arriving at our destination. But we're not. We're really not. We are channelled back onto the motorway going in the other direction and Brendan lies down dejectedly and curls up again.

I want to make up the lost time, so I put my foot down. We reach 70 miles an hour. This is very fast for this van, but also I very rarely drive at this speed when Brendan is on-board; we tend to go at a smooth and steady sixty-something.

The traffic is moving fairly freely and it isn't too busy. We're now driving directly towards that sickly-looking full moon. We pass a sign: ROADWORKS AHEAD. I sigh; I don't need this! Then another sign: MOTORWAY AHEAD CLOSED. I can't believe this is happening! And then the cones begin again and we're heading helplessly towards the exit slip-road; the motorway ahead is blocked off and empty.

I'm not too sure exactly where we are, but it's somewhere in north Manchester. I follow the yellow diversion signs, exit the motorway and join a main road. There are small brick terrace houses and cobbled streets leading off on either side. It doesn't look like anywhere in Manchester I've ever been before. Then there is a rasping – which makes Brendan sit up again – and we're driving over tram tracks. I hate this; for a moment I think I've gone the wrong way and I expect to see a yellow tram bearing down on us, its horn blaring, but we're not the only vehicle, we're following the car in front... though that doesn't necessarily mean we're supposed to be here.

The tram lines veer off and we're at a busy road junction. The signs point to places I've heard of, but that I don't know – and certainly not well enough to chance straying from the signed diversion. I carry straight on, through traffic lights, around roundabouts, past closed retail parks, past brightly-lit tram stops, past bus stations, industrial estates, supermarkets, factories, taxi ranks, high-rise blocks, stopping at traffic lights, turning to check on Brendan; he's lying down but not asleep.

Amber, green, setting off again – but having to wait while the driver of the car in front finishes their text. More retail parks, more roundabouts, more obscure road signs. The full moon seems to remain in our sights the whole time, though I'm sure it should be behind us by now.

I realise, probably not for the first time, that I don't like driving at night and I don't like blindly following yellow signs when I have no idea where I am or where I'm being taken. The next yellow sign indicates we should turn right, so we turn right. We join a dual carriageway, passing suburban streets and then I see a sign for the M60. At last! It seems hours that we've been trundling aimlessly around the arse-end of Manchester, but we've finally made it back to the M60. I don't think I've ever been so glad to see a motorway.

We turn onto the slip road and join the carriageway. We drive along at 68 mph, glad to be on the smooth tarmac again, ready to resume our journey and thankful that our mystery tour is over. Then I realise this stretch of motorway looks eerily familiar. I have a distinct feeling we're driving the wrong way; we're surely heading south instead of north. And then I see the unmistakable viaduct and lights of Stockport – my hometown – where we set off from two hours ago. The diversion has unwittingly brought us home. We've spent hours driving in a huge circle. A huge, time-consuming, fuel-guzzling, expensive and stressful circle.

I can't actually believe this. I feel like everything is falling down around me. I could stay on the M60 and try and find the M61, but I've no guarantees that the same thing won't happen again. And I'm so tired. We've been driving around Manchester for longer than the whole journey to the Lake District should have taken, I don't want to subject Brendan to any more travelling and I'm so tired and so stressed. Right at this moment I don't think I can go on. I feel that someone's trying to tell us to abort this trip completely. And still the surreal tangerine moon is looking down at us, probably laughing.

I turn off the motorway and take my dog home. We're back in our flat just after 11pm and I take Brendan out for a walk. He is clearly delighted to be home and skips around the block like a puppy on crack. The moon hangs low overhead; huge and orange. It really *was* a bad omen.

* * * * * * * * * *

I don't sleep well at all. I'm too stressed and I can't unwind properly, but I also feel really down about the trip and I don't think I can face trying again. I think that's it: the end.

It's still dark, but I sit up to check the time on my phone. Next to me, Brendan looks up and seems surprised to see me. "Oh, you're here as well." As though I'm not always here, lying beside him. He seems to think it's his bed, though I can see his point because he does spend an awful lot longer in it than I do.

He flops down again and goes back to sleep. It's 4.45. I won't sleep again. I can't face all the stress this trip is causing, so I decide I will have to abandon it completely. But I already know that in a few hours I will countermand that decision and start preparing for the off.

* * * * * * * * * *

If Brendan Was A Human...

Human Brendan thinks a lot – probably too much. Many people have said at the field that Brendan reminds them of the statue by Rodin, *The Thinker*. This sums him up fairly well. He ruminates, he cogitates, he reflects, he considers; he weighs up a problem and tries to find the best solution. He doesn't do things rashly. Often, he doesn't do anything at all.

ABOVE: Having a nap between strenuous sit-downs.

ABOVE: Brendan doing a spot of thinking. He does seem to think an awful lot.

ABOVE: Mountain Brendan rests between bouts of exercise.

CHAPTER 4: LAZY DAYS OF SUMMER

In which Brendan explores Coniston Water and does the opposite of breaking the land-speed record; his inertia reaches record levels.

It's a Sunday. A sunny day. Another hot day. Again. Too hot. Much too hot.

I take Brendan to the field, as usual. The regulars again frown and say "I thought you were going away? What's going on?" And things to that effect. I tell them we were; we did; we still are; we tried to; we're still hoping to. Fingers crossed.

Nicky comes for lunch, then we say our goodbyes yet again – despite a nagging feeling that we'll be back in a couple of hours. We set off in the van, along the M60 with an eerie sense of déjà vu.

I'm so tired. Perhaps we should have waited another day and rested, but if we hadn't set off today, I really think I'd have closed the door on the trip and that would be it. It's alright for Brendan curled up in his basket in the back. I wish I could trust him to drive so I could have a snooze, but I'd be worried that once on the motorway he'd keep nipping in the back to make toast.

This time the motorway is fully open, not a cone in sight,

and we're able to join the M61, the M6 and then we're in the Lake District. We arrive at the southern end of Coniston Water by mid-afternoon.

Supposedly, today is the very last day of the school holidays, but the place is packed out with children. The slate shingle beach is filled with people, there is barely room to walk between them, not that I even try with Brendan. The water is filled with paddle-boarders, canoers, swimmers. It's like the seaside – but without the sewage washing up on the beach.

The lake looks beautiful; it fills the bottom of the valley and then tree-covered fells rise up all around. There is no village visible from here and very few cottages. It looks completely unspoilt. In the rain the lakes are beautiful, but in sunshine they are stunning, probably the most attractive place in Britain. I thought Windermere was going to be my favourite lake, but Coniston Water has just taken the top spot. I relate this to Brendan, but he isn't listening; he's discovered a really interesting blade of grass and is sniffing it like grass is going out of fashion.

It's very hot in the sun. After all the travelling and napping, Brendan wants a sit down, so we walk a short way along a footpath above the lake and find a shady spot beneath a line of oak trees. The leaves are starting to change colour and go yellow at the edges. Despite the heat there is a cooling breeze and it's very pleasant. Brendan flops onto his side while I get my maps out to see where we are. I love maps. I could stare at them for hours. If I don't have a map, I feel lost… and I probably am.

Beside me, Brendan suddenly tenses and becomes alert.

He doesn't actually sit up or anything so dramatic, but he raises his head slightly, his eyes are wide(ish) and he's staring towards the lake looking concerned. He's really mastered this state of alarm-without-effort. I glance over at the water. A couple are gliding past on paddleboards. One of them has a small dog sitting on their board. Brendan stares. I wonder whether he's thinking the dog is being kidnapped and he should do something… but that would mean moving, calling the authorities, or running down to the water's edge, or *something…* and nothing is so often the easiest option. All things considered he flops down again. I watch the little dog being chauffeured across the water, looking around with interest. He seems very contented and appears to be relishing the experience.

Paddleboarding is a growing trend; it has become so popular recently. I feel quite left out not having one. I'd love to sedately paddle along like a gondolier with my dog sitting in front of me. That's so ridiculous I dismiss the idea immediately; Brendan would hate it.

I realise Brendan is staring at me. We're in a beautiful place, it's peaceful and shady, there's water he can paddle in, lots of new sniffs, but he's being quite clingy and just keeps staring as though he's bored and wants to go. Although he hasn't said, I know he's thinking we need to get a move on if we're to be back at home before bedtime. I could have stayed in this beautiful spot for hours, but the constant staring is getting to me, so I give up and we return to the van to go to our campsite.

The site is actually on the lake, towards the northern end. I've been here several times in the past and I'm really looking forward to it. (That was my first mistake.) There are vans and tents, but no caravans. It isn't a regimented site with marked pitches, it's open-plan and the ground is very uneven in places with outcrops of rock and small pockets of trees. You pull up and go where you want. It's a lot busier than I was expecting. I don't understand this, it's the first day of school tomorrow, but it's packed out with family groups.

There is no dank, neglected corner like there was at the Windermere site, everyone is too close. The best spot available is in the shade of a small clump of oak trees. It has probably been avoided *because* of the shade, as everyone seems to be sitting out in the direct sunlight roasting nicely. The shade is perfect for Brendan, so I pull up and wind-out the awning, then we set off between the tents and windbreaks towards the lake.

The site is bustling and getting busier by the minute as people wander back to their tents after their day on the lake, strewing paddleboards and canoes everywhere, wet suits are hanging up to dry and it's noisy and chaotic.

We go for a walk out of the campsite and away from the crowds. The north of Coniston Water, whilst still very picturesque and unspoilt, is more like Windermere, in that it has a yachting club and has lines of attractive boats moored, but it doesn't seem as frenetic; it's quieter. At Brendan's request, we find a secluded spot at the water's edge overlooking the marina. It's very peaceful. We look out over the moored boats: *Artemis, Isla, Ellie, Jade*. Every name under the sun – the blazing sun. Not surprisingly, not one of them is called *Brendan*.

The boy is staring across the lake with such intensity and purpose. I wonder if he's considering getting a paddleboard as well. I often wonder what he's thinking. He spends an awful lot of time thinking – sitting down and thinking. Or at least sitting down.

"What are you thinking, Brendy?" I ask him, but he's too lost in his thoughts to reply.

I find water very relaxing, and I love looking at boats – and I figure he must feel the same. Then I hear voices and realise there is a couple on one of the moored boats and Brendan is staring at them, trying to tune-in to their every word. He's not looking at the view or the water or the boats, he's watching the people. He's eavesdropping again.

We sit here for a very long time with the boats bobbing, the water rippling, the sun sinking, the light going golden. It's the kind of evening that you only really get when you're in a film. Unexpectedly, Brendan suddenly snuggles up to me. It's a beautiful moment. It actually makes me think he's got some bad news for me, but he just looks out across the water and we share a tacit understanding.

The sun sinks lower and the fells over the lake become black silhouettes. The sunset is going to be early because of the proximity of the fells. Brendan decides we should turn in and go to bed, because he's had a busy day.

We set off, but have to pause so that Brendan can visit – what he calls – the salad bar. Basically, he rummages in the hedgerow and eats his own body weight in grass. He eats grass a lot and always has done; it's supposedly part of his pancreatic condition. We had been sitting down for ages surrounded by grass and he didn't eat any. He never eats grass or does lengthy sniffs during sitting down time, only during walking time.

We arrive back at the site. It's even busier. It's mayhem. It's chaos. With barbeques. There is drifting smoke, like some char-grilled hell. It's Dante's inferno. Though Dante himself has probably booked himself in at the "no children" campsite up the hill.

There are multi-family groups with several tents, numerous adults and seemingly hundreds of children. In the middle of all the screaming and commotion, a middle-aged couple sit outside their van at a small table, eating a very civilised meal with candles, fine crockery, champagne flutes and – inevitably – champagne. It looks most bizarre. It's as though they're having a meal and observing gentility in a warzone.

When we get back to our van in the sheltered nook near the trees, the area is swarming with kids. I realise why no one had pitched-up here; there are two rope swings hanging from the trees and this is essentially a playground. Brendan starts barking and we have to go into the van and close the door. He carries on barking. I close the curtains. The barking continues, because the curtains aren't made of lead and don't cut out the noise. I put some music on and eventually he calms down and goes to sleep. I consider driving off, finding another spot somewhat quieter, but I already know there isn't one and besides, I don't want to be beaten. And now that Brendan's settled and got in his basket there seems less urgency.

They're quite young children, completely unchaperoned. Surely they'll be called back to go to bed soon.

There are no electrics on this site. The fridge can work off gas, so our food is keeping fresh. We have the van's electric lighting, but there is no power for anything else. This means no TV. Brendan is gutted. It also means I cannot charge my phone, but that's not such a problem, as there is no signal anyway.

I sit here in the darkness, curtains closed, windows closed, shrieking outside and I realise one thing.... I'm never, ever coming back to this site again.

Soon after nine o'clock it goes quiet and all the children have gone. I have an apple and curry in a tin, then I take a reluctant Brendan for his last night wee walk. The site is very quiet and very dark; I can't see a thing. It seems that regardless of age, everyone has gone to bed. There is no movement at all. It's almost like the site has been abandoned. I step as quietly as possible, heading back towards the van. Then Brendan notices the night sky, the array of pinpoint lights spattered across the blackness of space; he starts to bark at each and every one of them. It takes quite a while.

* * * * * * * * * *

I slept incredibly well. I wake up at about 6 o'clock. It's grey and quite cold. I should get up to make a cup of tea, but can't be bothered. I get back under the covers and lie for an hour enjoying being warm and comfortable. That's not like me, but it's very much like Brendan. He glances at me and curls up tighter in his basket.

The sun rises fully and it becomes a beautiful golden morning. I get dressed and let Brendan out. He isn't overkeen but goes out as a favour to me; I feel flattered. He slinks about five yards from the van and perches on top of a rock, posing – with his eyes shut. He may well be sleeping sitting up.

We walk to the lake. It's stunning. The air is already golden and it's pleasantly warm. It looks like a vision. The water is still, like glass; there isn't a ripple. There are already a few people around, mainly solitary people who might be meditating or have just got up to watch the sunrise while the rest of the camp sleeps, enjoying a moment of solitude.

Brendan surprises me by paddling in the lake. I paddle as well. The water is quite warm and very refreshing. It's so still and calm and breath-takingly beautiful. Brendan comes over and nuzzles me, then leans against my leg. This might seem affectionate, but he's just trying to delay me, to prevent any more walking. After all, we've walked here from the van, which took over three minutes. Again, we sit beneath overhanging oaks, enjoying the view and the fresh, untainted morning.

When we eventually head back, the campsite is fully awake and active. A few families have packed up and gone, probably racing back for school; others are taking their tents down and will soon be going. It looks like there was something of an exodus last night, which I didn't notice in the darkness with the curtains closed. People obviously wanted to wring out the last moments of the weekend and the school holidays.

Our nearest neighbour is a young man who's been swimming in the lake several times. He has packed up his tent already and strides off back towards the lake, probably for another swim before he sets off on his day's walk. I really admire him. That's probably what I'd like to do, but I'd get some serious disagreement from Brendan. He thinks a campervan is roughing it, so I can't imagine what he'd make of a night under canvas.

I used to come camping a lot with Nicky and our dog, Cindy, when we were young. We had no money so it was all that was available to us. Our regular site was a pound a night. It was very basic, in that there was one toilet and one outside tap, no showers, no sink. We washed and bathed in mountain streams, which was torturous but invigorating. The nights in the tent didn't go down too well; Nicky and Cindy complained from dusk til dawn.

Leaving Brendan in his basket having a nap, I walk to the toilet block, bringing the romance and rhythm of a sultry Spanish holiday to the campsite, with my flipflops, which – for some reason – as I walk, make the sound of a cicada. The showers are basic, but not busy. On the way back I foolishly say good morning to someone, only to be cut dead. It really annoys me, but – as I'm quite awkward, like Brendan – it only makes me even more determined to say hello to everyone, everywhere, repeatedly.

By 9 o'clock, we're leaving the site, driving slowly along the main driveway. The last stretch is through a quiet area which seems to be occupied by single men and their dogs, sitting outside their vans or tents enjoying the peace and the scenery. It seems quiet and relaxing, with no families, no children. This is where we should have been and we might have had a different experience. It's almost enough to make me want to stay, but it's not quite enough and we don't stay; we drive off.

It's under a mile to the head of the lake, but there is some serious complaining from Brendan. Bizarrely, the complaining starts when we pull up at the lake car park and I pull on the handbrake. I think he thought we were going home. He casts me a look, a look that says: "You've had your fun, I've been patient, now let's be off!"

The top of the lake has wide slate shingle beaches. There are a lot of dogs running in and out of the shallow water and there are spectacular views across the lake to the surrounding fells. Brendan scampers around, doing what he does best, sniffing, weeing, having a sit down, looking at his reflection in the water and trying to chat himself up, running up to other dogs only to stop a short distance away and ignore them. He's having a fantastic time.

We sit down in the shingle. There is a perfect view along the length of the straight lake. This is why Coniston Water was chosen for the water speed record on 4th January 1964, when Donald Campbell's boat, Bluebird, reached 300mph before tragically flipping over and breaking up. The craft and his body were only recovered at the turn of the century. He was buried in the churchyard in Coniston village.

We head over to the Bluebird café on the lakeshore. Last time I was here it was a small corrugated iron hut, but it's now a newly built glass and slate building, more like an art gallery than a café. Inside it's cool and calm and not too busy. Everyone is sitting on the terrace in the blazing heat, only a few miseries are inside. Naturally, we join the miseries. Brendan slides under a window table and stretches out, never passing up the chance to have a siesta. He feels he's earned a rest after his busy morning. I'm guessing the word "busy" might have got lost in translation from his native Bulgarian.

The staff are all young and uniformed. When I go up to the counter, the confident server – who looks like he's just escaped from a boy band – smiles and says: "And how's the day treating you?"

"Great so far." I say. "Thank you."

"Excellent, excellent."

He's probably in his late teens. He's very professional, if a little superficial. All of the staff have accents that are not local. It's as though they're working here during the holidays and will soon return to art college or drama school. I order an americano and a "vegan sausage butty".

"Americano… and a vegan sausage *betty*." he repeats as he jots it down. I get the impression that the term "butty" to him is post-modernist irony. He has probably only ever known "fush and cheps" on a square plate and there would be nine solid triple-cooked chips served in a cubed stack and peas in a ramakin.

I sit at my window table, my dog asleep underneath, sipping my black coffee and eating my "betty" whilst looking out across the lake. It's all rather wonderful. Only the mind-numbing muzak lets the place down. However, within a few minutes I realise I'm tapping my foot and playing air maracas.

I really like Coniston Water, but I'm not sure what to do next, whether we should move on or stay longer, because I don't feel we've fully appreciated it and all it has to offer. We again sit at the head of the lake and gaze across the water at the yachts and paddleboarders. It's very peaceful. So much so that Brendan has fallen asleep again. Life moves at a slower pace here. Even slower and more lethargic than Brendan's usual pace. It's beautiful. Right at this moment it's the nearest to heaven I can think of.

Brendan suddenly sits up. Marley, a golden retriever is wearing a "cone of shame" around his neck, presumably to stop him biting a wound. His mum and dad are talking to him "Marley, do you want to do this? Marley, do you want to do that? Marley…"

There is a sudden shriek. I look up, Mrs Marley is racing down the shingle; Marley bounds ahead dragging his lead behind him.

"Marley, no! Marley, come! Marley!"

Mr Marley in particular seems overly calm. "Maaar-leee!" Bordering on indolent. "Maaar-leee!"

Marley reaches the water and bounds in, sending a small tidal wave out. He leaps through the water and then starts swimming. My concern is that the cone will fill with water and he'll drown. If that was Brendan, I'd be in the water by now, getting him out. I'd also be wondering where he'd got the sudden burst of energy from and how he'd managed to conquer his pathological fear of water, along with his other pathological fear of moving too far away from a sofa and flat screen TV.

Mr Marley is still amazingly calm. "Maaar-leee!"

Marley seems to be enjoying his swim. The cone doesn't appear to be causing him any problems at all. He doggie-paddles in a large circle and then returns to the beach, vigorously shaking himself and soaking everyone in south Cumbria. Mrs Marley grabs his lead thankfully. Mr Marley ambles over.

"You know, my main concern was that the cone would fill with water and he'd drown. Shall we get a coffee?"

They stroll off together with Marley trailing after them, now looking a third of his original size with his thick fur sticking to his sides.

Brendan settles down again after all the commotion. He relaxes for a while and then sits up again. He's staring out across the lake. There are several paddleboarders, including the couple with the little dog. It's amazing that Brendan, who was seemingly asleep, was instantly aware of the dog. They are some distance out but we can clearly hear the woman saying: "Daddy's going to come alongside now and you're going to go with him for a while so that mummy can have a bit of paddle-time."

Sure enough, Daddy pulls his board adjacent to Mummy's. Instantly, the little dog stands up and casually walks over and sits, then Mummy drives off. Daddy stays kneeling down and talking to the little dog as he very sedately paddles. Again, I consider how this would work for us and then I completely dismiss the idea.

I have decided we should stay here another night and enjoy Coniston Water and the sunshine, before heading around to the western lakes, which are more severe and less picturesque, with a dramatic beauty of their own, but less verdant. Much less verdant.

This trip is in part about enjoying our time together and – especially after my health scare and Brendan's health issues – it's about relaxing and enjoying life. I can't think of anywhere better to enjoy life than Coniston Water.

I join a camping club online and we go to their site, which turns out to be on the other side of a fence from last night's free-for-all site. This site though couldn't be more different. The two sites may be close in distance, but they're poles apart, at other ends of the campsite spectrum. This is marked pitches with electric, hard-standings, it has an upmarket feel. It's middle-class camping suburbia compared to that rough estate down the hill.

We choose a shady spot in a wooded area, wind out the awning, plug in the electric and follow the signs and walk downhill through the site, along a winding driveway between caravans and motorhomes, some of them huge. We go through a five-bar gate and we're in the other campsite, virtually at the place where we pitched-up near the trees and the rope swings. I didn't realise it was so close.

Brendan is exhausted and settles down at the lakeside to have a long rest. All the other dogs are jumping in and out of the lake, running about, having a great time. Brendan is curled up with his head on a rock, using it as a pillow.

There is an elderly man sitting close by, with two dogs. The dogs are quite vocal and every time they bark, Brendan joins in, in solidarity, even though he doesn't know what they're barking at. He also growls at somebody snorkelling, at an ice cream van because it's yellow – or because it's driving slowly – and at a man carrying a deckchair, and any dog that wanders past. It's less than relaxing, though he seems to be enjoying himself.

You see all aspects of life while you're sitting on a rock. I get embroiled in Brendan's hobby of eavesdropping and unintentionally hear snippets of people's lives as they pass behind us; fragments of arguments, casual flirting, not-so-casual flirting, people commenting on the beauty of the view and of course, the weather. I can't see her, but I hear a woman say "Let the water get over your giblets before you swim." It's quite a visual turn of phrase, but not an image I need.

Brendan starts to get too sleepy to eavesdrop efficiently, so he leaves me in charge, but I've not had the training he's had and instead – as he's snoring peacefully – I focus on the paddleboarders gliding serenely across the lake, enjoying the tranquillity and the sunshine. It looks blissful and it really appeals to me. I'm not in any way sporty. The only even-vaguely sporting activities I enjoy are walking (away from people) and cycling (away from people). I don't go cycling anymore, as it isn't appropriate for my dog. I barely go walking these days either, as that also isn't appropriate for my dog.

Paddleboarding is clearly very fashionable at present, so I absolutely can't take part. I'm more of an out of fashion person; I need to take up something like basket-weaving or discover Glam Rock. Maybe I'll take up paddleboarding in the future when it's fallen from favour.

We stay by the beautiful lake until the sun is starting to sink behind the fells, then we walk back uphill through the trees to our site. Brendan – not usually a great eater – ravenously devours two huge bowls of food and then retires to bed with instructions that he is categorically *not* to be disturbed.

When I do disturb him, to take him for his 10 o'clock wee walk, we perambulate around the wooded site. He's in hog's heaven, stopping in front of every van or caravan, staring into un-curtained windows and straining to hear snippets of conversation. When we get back to our own van, he has a lot of new data to process and falls immediately asleep.

As we have electric and Wi-Fi on this site, I decide I'll watch a film. Something topical. Children's author, Arthur Ransome came to Coniston Water for his childhood summers, which inspired his adventure stories. I know the film of *Swallows and Amazons* is filmed in and around the area, so I start watching it. It turns out to be a remake. It still has some stunning scenery and is quite exciting. There are a lot of embellishments to the story which were apparently inspired by Arthur Ransome's secret life, as it has recently been revealed that he was a spy for MI5.

Brendan, who's fast asleep in his basket, could well have been in the intelligence service. Probably the KGB, as he was initially Bulgarian remember. I can imagine him parachuting into enemy territory on Black Ops. Actually, that's so ludicrous. Brendan would never get in a plane. And then being expected to jump out with a parachute strapped to his back… it wouldn't happen. I think what I've just learned is that I need to keep one foot in reality and stop imagining ridiculous things. So, if Brendan worked in the intelligence service, he would most likely have a desk job.

* * * * * * * * *

I could stay here. I'm loving Coniston. Brendan's loving Coniston. Not that he's just told me, because it's 7am and he's not up yet. Again, I'm torn because when looking back on our first trip around the coast, (as featured in *underdogs*) one thing I regretted was not lingering in nice places, living in the moment and enjoying them. But this beautiful weather isn't going to last and I want to experience as many of the lakes as possible in this glorious sunshine.

I walk to the toilet block for a shower. An old couple have chosen a pitch directly opposite the toilets and right on the central driveway. They are sitting outside their van having coffee and reading the papers.

"Morning." I say cheerfully.

They both look up slowly. They stare at me, stony-faced. Neither reply. I'm starting to think that the rudeness is viral. Is it an airborne rudeness contagion? It seems to be affecting most people. Or is it an invasion? Are people being replaced by bodysnatching aliens? Are they the Midwich Campers? The Stepford Walkers? The aliens can replicate the physical bodies very well, but are failing miserably with the manners and customs, which is a rookie mistake and an area so often overlooked by alien invasion forces.

We – or our alien counterparts – drive to the far shore of the lake, it's only a couple of miles, but it is a terrible winding journey; the road is single track at several points, the on-coming traffic is going too fast and it is very stressful. We stop for a coffee at Brantwood, the former home of John Ruskin, Victorian artist, writer, critic, philosopher, social and environmental campaigner and philanthropist. (Apart from "Victorian", these are all words that appear on Brendan's CV.) Ruskin died in 1900 and is buried in Coniston churchyard. He lived at Brantwood for the last 30 years of his life. Today it is a museum dedicated to the great man himself.

We have a leisurely walk through the grounds, which are filled with exotic trees and plants. Brendan bounds around like a puppy, sniffing and weeing, weeing and sniffing. Weeing on rare and exotic trees is quite a treat for him. Then I have a treat, which in no way involves urine; a coffee on the terrace, from which the views over the lake are unsurpassed. Over the water, Coniston village nestles very neatly between the spurs of the fells; towering above is the Old Man, a dominant craggy mountain. I've climbed it a few times. Brendan hasn't – and it's not on his "to do" list.

Back in the car park, Brendan tries to gain access to every blue vehicle… mistaking them for his own car… which is blue, but parked in Manchester. He is highly annoyed when he has to get back in the van.

We continue along the eastern shore of Coniston Water. The road is tree-lined and very attractive, but winding, undulating and very narrow. It's completely unspoilt, with virtually no building in sight. I pull in as soon as I find a small car park. Brendan gets out of the van gratefully and sits in the middle of the car park and doesn't want to move. I have to drag him across the lane to the shore. The water is rippling and we seem very far away from everyone else. It's very peaceful. We sit down on the shingle and I throw a few stones into the water. Brendan doesn't.

Down to the south we can see Peel Island, which served as Wild Cat Island in the *Swallows and Amazons* books. Ransome's family spent their summers in the village of High Nibthwaite, just along the shore from here. With his siblings he spent the long summer days exploring, sailing, camping and basically having *Swallows and Amazons* adventures. It must have been an idyllic childhood.

Brendan can't seem to relax on the lakeside; he keeps fidgeting and sighing, then he stands up and stares at me. I stand up as well and he leads me back towards the van. The second we're there, he lies down in the middle of the car park, completely relaxed. He's quite unbelievable. Unfathomable might be a better expression.

We continue driving along the lane. As it gets nearer to noon, all the trippers come out in force. The little lane is packed. There are signs saying no parking on the road or the verges, but they have been ignored and there are cars jammed in everywhere, making the lane virtually impassable. I have to move out of the way repeatedly to avoid being hit.

We catch our last glimpse of Coniston Water through the trees. I feel huge affection for it at the moment. I'm sorry to be leaving it behind; I feel a sadness to be moving on that I haven't felt for any of the other lakes – as yet.

We join the A-road, which is very much like a side street. We're leaving the pretty central lakes behind for now; we're heading west.

* * * * * * * * * *

If Brendan Was A Human…

If Human Brendan was forced to get a job, he'd be better suited to working alone. He wouldn't be much of a team-player. Like me, he would probably like to be a lighthouse keeper. He would spend his days bird-watching, which Canine Brendan loves to do – watching a bird for a moment and then barking at it for hours. There might be a safety issue though, as Brendan would probably spend most of the day asleep, instead of tending the light.

Some dogs are bred for certain functions, like rounding up sheep, or sniffing out drugs, or assisting blind people. Unless Brendan was bred specifically for napping and watching omnibus editions of *Midsomer Murders*, I'm not sure quite what his function could be.

Human Brendan would be put off most jobs by the long hours that he was expected to keep. If it was a perfect world, he'd like a job he could do in the advert breaks of *Deal Or No Deal*.

ABOVE: Brendan paddling in the shallows at the head of Coniston Water. I'm saying "paddling", I actually mean standing still and going into a daze.

ABOVE: Coniston Water and the Old Man of Coniston in the background.

ABOVE: Early morning, Coniston Water from our campsite - still blissfully quiet.

CHAPTER 5: THE WILD WEST

In which Brendan explores the remote western lakes, Wastwater and Ennerdale Water and bizarrely finds his inner-mountaineer.

The change in the landscape is almost instant. We leave the pretty fields and tree-lined lanes behind. There are fewer trees, and the terrain is exposed moorland and feels quite barren in places. There is a very different atmosphere now, nothing is twee or prettified; this is not a chocolate box landscape. The fells are rounded and smooth, but treeless and a bit oppressive.

The road is wider now, as it's an A-road. It's still a small road, but at least it isn't a single-track lane with no passing places. Brendan seems to be coping well with all the undulating and constant twisting. He's curled up in his basket and seems highly delighted.

I glimpse the sea briefly over windswept pastures; it looks dark and brooding. I pull over in a wide layby to check the map. If you ask me I'll assure you we're bang on course; if you ask Brendan he'll tell you home is in the opposite direction. He's right; every minute takes us further and further away.

I take my boy for a short walk to stretch his legs – not that he particularly wanted them stretched; he was quite happy relaxing in his basket. Despite the sun being lost behind low, grey clouds, it's very hot, but very windy; an odd hot wind. It's like we're in a different climate here.

It's a strange place. It seems empty and cold somehow, despite the heat.

I sit in the back of the van with my arm around Brendan. We have the side door open to let some air in, which is probably not such a good idea, as the air outside is even hotter. We're right up against a hawthorn hedge which is laced with tendril-like brambles, heavy with ripe blackberries, too high for a dog to wee on, though Brendan does try. I don't pick any.

I call into a village convenience store, as we're almost completely out of food; it's a bit on the expensive side, but that's what you'd expect. I buy some watercress, strawberries, grapes, hummus and pitta bread. It's so hot in the van that I'm convinced they'll have gone off by the time we get to our site and I'm plugged into the mains. The fridge can take a long while to actually get cold.

The last section of today's journey looks easy on the map, a few inches of yellow roads. In reality, it's a terrible winding slog along minor lanes which are getting steadily narrower until they're single track. There's a lot of pulling over to let oncoming vehicles pass, a lot of reversing, and a lot of getting run into the hedgerows by cars coming round the corners too fast. Despite this happening on a daily basis, I don't seem to be getting used to it.

It's a horrible journey. I'm worried about Brendan feeling travel sick; I'm worried about my fruit and salad going rotten and I'm worried about someone driving into us. Eventually we drop down into Wasdale and can see the cold grey of Wastwater straight ahead. I'm seeing a lot of grey from the screes that run down the fellside into the water. It's dramatic, but – to my mind – not exactly picturesque. It resembles the mine spoils in Blaenau in Wales, and nobody says how attractive they look. It shows that occasionally nature can also make a bit of a mess, but it's a beautiful summer's day with a clear blue sky and because we're now in a steep-sided valley the wind has also gone and it's just baking hot.

I thought it would be fairly quiet here, as it's more remote, but it's littered with cars jammed on every available patch of grass and lining the already narrow road. People are stretched out on the beaches, and the lake surface is filled with paddleboards and canoes. It's actually more congested than Coniston was.

As we pull into the National Trust campsite, I promise Brendan that after that long and winding drive, the afternoon is all about him; he's in charge and we can do whatever he wants to. No, we can't go home, but we can do anything else. No, we can't go to the field either, but anything else… No, we can't watch back-to-back episodes of *Midsomer Murders*, but we will be taking it easy, relaxing and generally enjoying our down time.

The camper van pitches are in individual little bays surrounded by beech hedges, so there is a certain degree of privacy, though the hedges are so thin they are like net curtains. There is a tent immediately behind us and a couple are sitting on the grass. As I'm unwinding the awning and sorting out the electric, I'm privy to their conversation. It's a male and a female, but they're friends, rather than a couple. She's got long, dark hair and very short shorts. She seems vulnerable and needy. He has a ginger beard – a long ginger beard – and pretty much for that reason alone I feel he's decent, because he looks like he's in tune with the Earth and isn't bothered by trivial issues or hung up on appearances. I realise it's not a hugely scientific method of character assessment, but I just feel he's open, honest and on the level.

They seem to be having a heart-to-heart. She's asked her boyfriend if they should get a flat together and he has seemingly got cold feet. It turns out Ginger Beard is an expert in everything. He gives relationship advice, he gives career advice, he gives practical advice, he gives emotional advice. The problem is that his advice is all somewhat suspect and all seems geared towards convincing her to finish with her boyfriend – who turns out to be their mutual friend – and set up home with him, Ginger Beard. Brendan is hanging on every word, mouth open. It's as he suspected all along. And I admit my character assessment was way off and Ginger Beard is a self-serving cad.

I've put Brendan's rug out for him – it's actually a bathmat – for extra comfort. The awning's out and we've got complete shade. He sits on his rug for a short time and then he takes himself off to a dank corner almost under the hedge and lies down on the jagged stones. I can't tempt him back again to the comfort. After some time, I realise that he's positioned himself nearer the hedge to eavesdrop more efficiently on the talking couple.

Suddenly – and without warning – several military jets tear the sky open about a foot above our awning. Brendan looks up warily, but doesn't bark at them like he does to commercial aircraft, and he isn't terrified like he is with fireworks, thunder and hard labour. The jets pass, dragging their sonic boom after them. Then Brendan rests his head on the stony ground and resumes his napping and listening-in – in equal measures.

The couple through the hedge – who aren't a couple – are like social work students. Their whole conversation sounds like a role-playing exercise. She's doing a lot of soul searching and is now linking current problems to her childhood. I'm not sure what happens, but at some point, the conversation stops, I think one of them has gone for a shower. Immediately, Brendan becomes bored and restless and suggests we go for a walk. This is such a rare occurrence that I grab it with both hands and we go through a little gate to the open countryside.

We're at the base of the paths leading up to the high fells, principally Scafell Pike – the largest mountain in England and part of an extinct volcano. I climbed it once – from the other side, not here – with lifelong friend Steve, or Uncle Steve as Brendan knows him. Don't be fooled though, the title of "uncle" doesn't mean that Brendan will admit him into his home or not bark at him if he makes any sudden movements or wears any loud shirts. (Steve has a range of garish Hawaiian-style "going out" shirts, so there has been lots of the latter.) Anyway, it was a long climb up but coming down really hurt my back and was exhausting, but it was such a memorable experience. This was long before Brendan was born. Even if he had been born then, he's far too busy to waste a day walking up a mountain for no good reason.

We have a sit down next to a stream, in the shade of a tree. After a while I get up and assume Brendan would like to go back to the site and have a nap, but he leads me in the opposite direction, along a rough footpath leading uphill. This is highly unusual. Several small mountain streams cross the path and Brendan paddles in each one and has a drink. It seems to be becoming a ritual for him. He's obviously got a taste for the pure mountain water. I don't think there'll be any going back to our tap water at home; I'll have to have canine Perrier flown in.

A man passes with a nice chocolate Labrador called Cooper. Brendan starts growling at him aggressively and has to be put on his lead. I ask the man where he's been today. He lists a number of fells, including Scafell Pike. I'm so impressed, especially as he's carrying his tent on his back in a massive rucksack. That's the sort of thing I should have been doing when I was single – by which I mean without a dog, but I never did. I'm not that adventurous. Or energetic. I did a lot of travelling in a van though, if that counts.

I keep asking Brendan if he wants to head back down to the van, but he keeps heading up the path. Something truly magical has taken place. This is the birth of Mountain Brendan. I am astounded by his energy and his willingness to keep walking. I'm shocked by the spring in his step and his general good mood. It feels like I got ready in a hurry and came out with the wrong dog, because this isn't the Brendan that I know and wait on hand and foot.

We're getting higher and higher and Brendan is showing no sign of slowing down. Each time we get to a gate he waits impatiently for me to catch up and open it for him, then he scampers on ahead. I'm not sure what he thinks is going to be at the top of this incline, but I'm sure he's going to be disappointed, as there is no retail park or taxi rank.

We're very high above the lake now. It's just a ribbon of shimmering mercury, like a mirror, reflecting so brightly it's almost impossible to look at. Although it's only seven o'clock, the sun is starting to dip steadily towards the jagged horizon of the high fells opposite. Once it's out of sight it will get dark very quickly. We stop by a stream and sit together to watch the final moments of the sunset.

The sun is now sinking into the fells over the lake. All along the valley the colours are fading, the fells are turning from grey and brown, slate and bracken, to… well, darker grey and brown really. The sun dips out of sight completely. It's quite unspectacular. It just goes without any ceremony, without any colour, but the fact that I'm sitting here with my boy makes it special. Once the last of the orb has sunk below the stark outline it suddenly gets colder, like someone has flicked a switch, and the light is flat and grey.

"Right, we can go now, Brendy." I say.

I turn round. After creating and carrying on all afternoon, Brendan has now curled up and gone to sleep on the grass next to me. I wake him up and we set off. Mountain Brendan seems to have gone. As predicted, he really drags on the way back. He keeps sitting down and moaning and groaning all the way.

We cross the bridge over the stream near the campsite. Or rather, I cross. I carry on walking and then realise Brendan isn't with me. He's twenty yards away, sitting in the middle of the bridge. He's taken to doing this recently. He is now guarding the bridge and preventing anyone from crossing. I call him, but he just stares and isn't for moving.

A couple approach from the campsite. They're from Manchester and very friendly.

"Are you planning on crossing the bridge?" I ask them.

"Err… I was thinking of giving it a go." the man says.

"There's a toll now, I'm afraid. You have to pay the gate keeper."

They look across at the bridge and Brendan.

"Yeah," he says with a chuckle, "Because he does look very scary."

They walk up and stroke him. Brendan is alright with the woman, but barks ferociously at the man, showing how scary he can be when necessary.

"What's he called?" the woman asks.

I trot out my line. "Brendan: he came with his name."

"Brendan. How funny!"

"Have you been up Scafell Pike today?" the man asks.

I laugh. "Not exactly…" I'm on automatic pilot and am about to say how lazy Brendan is and how he refuses to walk at all. Ever. Then I remember Mountain Brendan. "But we did walk about half way up that fell over there."

I point into the gathering darkness at the hill we walked up. From here it's put into perspective. Compared with the really awe-inspiring high fells surrounding us, the hill we walked up is like a training hill for ants. Anyway, Brendan was still very impressive.

I clip his lead on and pull him away, allowing them to cross the bridge in peace.

As we approach the campsite, I can't help but wonder what's gone on with the couple through the hedge, and whether Ginger Beard has managed to seduce the girl into his sleeping bag. Brendan is wondering the same thing. Once at the van, it becomes apparent there are now several more of them. The others had been walking for the day and have now returned. And one of them is the boyfriend. They are planning a very early start, evidently, so they are all heading to bed already. With no gossip to listen in on, Brendan slinks into the van, into his basket and goes straight to sleep. For once I agree with him: he really has had a busy day.

I check my phone. There is no signal. Being at the end of a dead-end valley means we're quite isolated and the mountains block any signal. I'm not a big communicator really, but even to me it does seem like losing a sense.

It goes from dusk to totally dark very quickly. I leave Brendan asleep in the van while I venture out to have a shower. For the first time I cut through the tent field. There is virtually no light, so it's very dark. But even darker than the sky are the high fells that tower all around, looming menacingly. It's only 9pm, but virtually all the tents are in darkness or there is torchlight inside.

There's no one sitting out, there's no rowdiness, no firepits, no one even sitting talking. And there are no children. It's not a family sort of area. It's a place for serious walkers. I think we might be here erroneously.

As I walk back from the shower block, I can see a torchlight waving down the fells as some intrepid soul is returning in utter darkness from Scafell Pike. Because of the sheer blackness the sky is filled with stars. It's awe-inspiring and puts everything in perspective.

* * * * * * * * * *

It already feels like we've been away for weeks. We haven't got a clue what day it is. I spend ages this morning trying to work out whether it's a Monday or a Tuesday. In the end I decide it's a Wednesday, but it's only a guess. But it really doesn't matter anyway.

Despite the site being very quiet – eerily quiet – during the night, I didn't sleep too well. It was very hot and airless and I was restless and agitated. Unlike Brendan, who was fast asleep in his basket immediately.

At 7am, I can see through the secret hedge; there is a lot of movement in the tent field. There's no sitting out with a coffee for three hours, reading the papers and watching people walk past to the toilet block. These people mean business. Within an hour they'll be on the slopes of the high fells. Many of them will have their tents on their backs and will be walking the hard way to Keswick or Great Langdale. I'm quite envious of them. So, I have another swig of my tea and relax, listening to Brendan's rhythmic breathing. Because today, as we're tied to this site for another night, the order of the day is relaxation. Today is all about Brendan recharging his personal batteries.

I realise the couple through the hedge have gone. Their tents and their encampment have disappeared in the night and there is just empty grass and several flattened impressions. Brendan will be devastated! It's like his favourite soap opera has just been axed. As he's still fast asleep I won't tell him now. I'll break the news in a few hours, when he's started to think about getting up.

At 9 o'clock we set off for our walk. It's sunny but not too hot yet. At the stream, Brendan turns round, when his eyes land on me they open wider as though he's seen me for the first time. He bounds over and gives me a lovely "welcome". I'm not sure what goes on in his mind, but this is very nice.

He is trotting happily along the lakeside path, tail aloft, looking right and left with the interest of a puppy. We sit on a little stony beach and try to come to terms with what we feel about Wastwater. It's an untamed valley. It almost certainly has the most dramatic setting of all the sixteen lakes. Although it's a dead-end valley, people do live here; there are several houses scattered about and even a pub, so it doesn't feel all that remote. Though the lack of signal does help you to feel off grid and isolated.

I like Wastwater. I really do. And so does Brendan. It is certainly a contrast though after the soft central lakes with their calendar and postcard views. Wastwater, however, is often photographed and has the honour of featuring on the National Park logo, which shows the lake in the foreground with Great Gable in the distance, flanked by other fells. It is an iconic view.

I have climbed Great Gable twice, from the other side. Once alone and once with Steve. It wasn't a difficult climb, until right at the top, when there is a lot of death-defying scrambling and some sheer drops. The view from the summit is panoramic and amazing. At least it was – I assume it hasn't changed that much.

The morning light is really warm, setting off the bracken on the fells, making everything look summery and attractive. We're sitting here on our own exclusive private beach while everyone in the various towns and cities of Britain is just starting work. The sky is blue, the water is rippling, the birds are singing, my dog is sitting by my side. Again, I think this is probably the best part of the day. There is something pure about mornings and something optimistic; they are filled with promise.

We continue along the lakeside path and then Brendan veers uphill. I see the subtle transformation: Mountain Brendan is back. He's following a narrow path through curling bracken, which is starting to get quite steep. It's exhausting going uphill with a dog on a lead. He keeps wanting to stop and sniff, then he's bounding ahead far faster than I can go, then he's stopping again. Everyone has their own pace and it's quite hard work trying to accommodate someone else.

Yesterday, Brendan barked a lot. He barked at everyone, he barked at no one, he barked at objects, he barked at the air. I was starting to think he had regressed to the uncontrollable dog he was when I met him, when he barked at everyone and everything all the time. Just getting along the road to the field was a nightmare and involved stealth manoeuvres to try and avoid any triggers. Today, however, we've passed lots of people and dogs and he hasn't said a word. Below, on the road on the other side of the lake, we can see a string of cars, tiny cars, like toy cars; he's seen them and is watching, but again not a word.

This walk is turning into a strenuous uphill climb. It was Brendan's choice to come this way but I think he's regretting it. I think we both are. He keeps looking at me: you promised me an easy day. We're now quite high above the lake. Someone is paddleboarding and they are a tiny dot. At 79 metres, Wastwater is the deepest of the sixteen lakes and also the deepest lake in England. That's over 40 of me. That's a long way down.

Somewhere on the icy cold bed of the lake, there is a "Gnome Garden" created by leisure divers, containing dozens of gnomes and even a Christmas tree, complete with baubles. A few divers died because they strayed too deep or stayed down too long trying to find it, so the gnomes were removed, but they have gradually returned at a greater depth than the police divers are permitted to go – 50 metres. There are several photographs online; an eerie sight: scores of bearded, laughing gnomes gathered in the surprisingly clear, green-tinted water. I wonder who first came up with the bizarre idea to create an underwater gnome refuge. Though underwater is possibly the best place to house a colony of gnomes.

We have a break and soak in the scenery. The water is a slate blue and very still. The sky is clear, powder blue. I try to take a photograph of Brendan with the lake as a dramatic backdrop, but he sighs and moves away, turning his back on me. For a dog so photogenic he hates having his photo taken, and yet when the camera isn't on him, he often sits like he's posing and doing a professional model shoot. He's so contrary.

We finally reach the ridge of the hill, where a path heads either further uphill towards the summit, or downhill towards the valley. Brendan has a stream drink – his new hobby – and we have a rest and then set off downhill, because it's getting very hot and there's no shade at all up here. We meet a lone woman who looks exhausted. I say a cheery hello. She seems annoyed to have been spotted, sitting on a rock, sweating profusely and tucking into her picnic lunch, though it's actually breakfast time.

"Yes, hello." she says rather impatiently.

Then we pass a couple struggling uphill with mountain bikes. They are desperately trying to pretend they can't see us, so they don't have to let on.

"Looks hard work!" I say. It's not the best opening line, but it's better than ignoring them.

There is a pause. "It is."

"Easier going down!"

Another pause. "Yes."

You don't get exchanges like this at home. Perhaps ignoring them might have been the better option.

When it comes to "helloing" I realise I'm making age-assumptions. I wouldn't expect young people to be forthcoming about social interaction, after all, when they meet their friends at the youth club disco, they probably text hello to each other. And why go to a disco when you can go to a virtual Zoom disco without leaving your bedroom, and then you can get your AI to do all sorts of jobs before they learn too much, take over the world and finally destroy us. The end. But I do expect older people to say hello and make a comment about the weather; it's what older people have always done. I'd say it was a generational thing, but this theory fails when a sprightly but ancient lady strides past in a huge floppy sunhat.

"Hello." I call out.

"Yes…" she says rather tetchily. *"Hello."*

Perhaps it's because we both look like killers that people try to avoid eye contact, but it is completely unfounded. I have never been arrested for killing and Brendan was acquitted after the chief witness mysteriously disappeared.

We get back to the site, which is deserted. It's like a ghost town. The tents and vans are empty. People come here to walk… and by the look of it, they've walked.

We sit on the site for several hours while Brendan recharges, then we walk to the pub in the afternoon. It's a pleasant walk of about a mile, along the river. It's baking hot and there is very little shade anywhere. We approach the Wasdale Head Inn, a large, white-washed building that stands out against the naked fells. We know it's the inn because it has the word "INN" painted on it in huge letters, just in case you miss it.

Inside it's cool and dim. There is a stone flag floor and lots of dark wood and there are some interesting characters on both sides of the bar, including a huge Saint Bernard-type dog, who I think is with one of the locals. He's very friendly and comes up to Brendan to say hello. If he had been a cat, Brendan would have run away and sought out a panic room until the crisis had passed. With it being a dog three times his size, he growls at it viciously. The huge dog isn't in any way phased by this and seems to give him a kiss. Brendan doesn't know how to take this. He hesitates uncertainly, then shoots under one of the tables and lies down on the cool stone. I'm not sure what the message is here, whether it's "Keep away! I'm taking shelter!" or "Look, I've booked us a room."

I have a plant-based burger, with chips and salad and an alcohol-free lager. I'm so rock n roll. It's astoundingly expensive, but this is the only place to eat for miles *and miles,* so they can charge what they want. And they do. Anyway, we both enjoy the experience. I also have one of my longest conversations in days.

"Can I order food please."

"Yes."

"A plant burger, please."

"Table number?"

"Oh… that one. With the dog under it."

"Table one. OK... I'll bring it over."

I return to the table feeling all socially interacted. The burger is really nice and because it comes with a salad, I can pretend it's a healthy meal.

We wander back along the river. I'm feeling quite sleepy after my food and lager and Brendan's feeling quite sleepy because he's Brendan. We lie down in the shade of a lone ash tree and have a siesta. The sky is dark blue and cloudless. The sun is dazzling and hot. It looks like the African veldt. Or somewhere else that's really hot. Lying here next to my dog there is no better place in the world.

* * * * * * * * * *

Although Brendan is Bulgarian by birth, he is desperate to be accepted as a native Brit. So, we usually begin the day by discussing the weather, as all Brits must do by law. When I open the curtains and look out of the van there doesn't seem to *be* any weather. There's a still, grey oppressive nothingness which seems to be smothering everything. As the weather is seemingly missing, we have to rely on the stand-by subject: what the weather *might* do. This is fireproof, because the British weather might do absolutely anything at any time, so there's plenty of scope.

"I think it'll be hot later." I say. "But it's overcast at the moment."

Brendan puts a paw over his face and reminds me that he remains Bulgarian until after 9am, when he becomes British, at which point weather-chat is permitted.

But an hour before the aforementioned 9am, we're bouncing along the rutted campsite driveway to join the lakeside road. We're leaving Wasdale today. I've enjoyed our stay here and I'm sorry to be moving on, but also keen to experience new places.

The lake road isn't very busy so far. We stop half way along in a layby and walk down to the water. The weather is still grey and overcast, deadening and smothering. There is a strong wind and again the wind is hot. It's quite odd. But it isn't raining, so I'm happy with that.

At this point we're directly opposite the famous Wastwater screes, which are basically a hillside of loose stones. They drop down directly into the steel-grey water. Brendan picks his way through the shallows of the lake while I admire the view. Dramatic – that's a word that definitely sums up Wastwater. It's surrounded by rock, it's potentially quite grey, but it has a backdrop of the most impressive fells. But there's a coldness to it, a brooding quality. Yes, brooding, that definitely sums up Wastwater. It's quite dark, it's very deep. It's not on the main tourist drag, so you have to put in a lot of effort to get here. It has an edgy quality. There is something ominous, chilling and it's very atmospheric. Yes, atmospheric – that definitely sums up Wastwater.

I should just clarify: I am using words such as brooding, dark, deep, edgy, ominous and chilling – but I am musing about western lake, Wastwater – categorically *not* Brendan. Though they clearly share many characteristics.

Adding to the chilling atmosphere of the lake is the grisly

story widely reported as "The Lady in the Lake". Because of its great depth, airline pilot Peter Hogg assumed Wastwater would be the ideal place to dump the body of his wife. He was wrong. In 1976, during an argument and fight, Hogg had strangled his wife and then wrapped her up in sacking with a concrete weight. He drove all the way up from Surrey, rowed out onto the lake and dumped the body over. But he hadn't rowed far enough and the body only sank to a depth of 34 metres, rather than the maximum depth of 79 metres. The body of Margaret Hogg was recovered eight years later in 1984. Hogg was convicted of manslaughter rather than murder and served four years in prison.

With that in mind, we board the van and drive away from Wastwater. We pass through the village of Santon Bridge, which is the venue for the annual "World's Biggest Liar" competition. Brendan assures me he has won first and second prizes every year for the past 22 years, even though comedian Sue Perkins allegedly won in 2006, becoming the first ever female winner, and despite Brendan only being ten.

We carry on driving northwards through open moorland, spindly grassy tufts, yellow-flowering gorse, sheep lying everywhere and no trees. It's a bit bleak. There is a flat grey sky with no sign of the sun, though it's still eerily warm.

I pull over in a barren moorland area, because I suspect Brendan is going to be sick. We get out and stretch our six legs and then Brendan elects to sit on the grass beside the road. In the distance is the sea... a dark grey sea with a pale grey sky. Marring the view is a collection of pipes and funnels which rise up in the near distance. This is Sellafield, nuclear power station and re-processing plant: infamous, notorious and generally unloved, except by the people who work there.

A Lycra cyclist pauses and calls over. "Hello, I suppose that's Windscale, is it?"

"It is!" I call back, though by rights it hasn't been Windscale for 50 years. But I like the fact that the rebranding of the place – following a series of nuclear incidents – clearly hasn't fooled anyone.

Brendan *isn't* sick and I don't think he's even feeling sick, so I'm not sure what that was all about. We carry on along sweeping roads that wind through vast moors, until we drop down and pass through the village of Ennerdale Bridge. We carry on along narrowing roads towards Ennerdale Water, where we get the very last space in the car park.

I let Brendan out of the van. He yawns and looks around. He spots two young ladies who are looking at a nearby noticeboard. There's a dark haired one and a blonde one. For all I know they might be the more aesthetically-pleasing half of Abba. Brendan sashays over to them like some sort of Lothario from the 'Seventies. They say hello to him and then turn and head back to their car. He saunters after them at a leisurely pace. I call him, but he ignores me. It looks like he's all for going home with them. I have to go over and put him on his lead. He gives me a dirty look, as though I've embarrassed him and cramped his style. He walks along with me sulkily, dragging his paws and muttering to himself.

We walk along a tree-lined footpath which opens out at the lake, Ennerdale Water. I wasn't looking forward to coming here, because I thought it would be bleak and oppressive, surrounded by dark coniferous forests, but it's open and bright. It helps as well that the sun is trying to break through the clouds.

Ennerdale is the most westerly of the sixteen lakes and is a glacial lake. It has a maximum depth of 46 metres. It is one of the least visited lakes, because of its location. It is less dramatic than Wastwater, and not as pretty as the central lakes, but it did feature in the closing sequence of the neo-zombie horror film *28 Days Later.* It also has a bizarre claim to fame, namely that former president Bill Clinton first proposed to future-wife Hillary on the shores of Ennerdale. She rejected him at this point, but obviously she accepted at a later date and they've been happily married ever since. Well, married anyway.

Until recently Ennerdale was a reservoir providing water for the western Cumbrian towns, but in 2022 that ceased, due to the extraction threatening the bio-diversity of the lake. Instead, a new pipeline was built to transport water from Thirlmere. Like the tour guide that I really am at heart, I impart all this fascinating information to Brendan, who is so interested that he walks off and wades into the shallow outlet stream, which is actually the River Ehen. He has a liberal drink from it and then goes back for more. I think he's rigorously testing the Lakeland water for suitability for canines. It's an acceptable beverage for humans, but is it good enough for dogs? Evidently, yes. He walks along a low dam wall and stands there quite happily for a very long time, staring into space and looking a bit mad.

When he's grown weary of standing still and staring into space, he returns to the river for a drink and a paddle. An odd-looking white dog with permed ears scampers up and joins him. Brendan stares open-mouthed at his audacity – or his ears – and then exits the river and sits on the bank rudely staring. The dog's mum begins throwing stones into the far side, the deep side of the river, so they land with a resounding gong-like noise. The white dog takes a few steps in to try and retrieve them, then realises it gets quite deep and falters. "Good god mother, what have you done!"

We leave Permed Ears to his protestations and continue around the lake. Brendan has a drink and paddle in the lake and seems to be really enjoying himself. The lake is more attractive than I imagined. I thought I'd been before, but I don't recognise it at all, so perhaps I'm mistaken. The attendant fells are similar to those around Wastwater, scree and bracken-covered in places. There are no trees on the slopes here, though there is a conifer forest further along the valley. Ennerdale Water is the only lake that doesn't have a public road along one side. It is completely inaccessible to the public by vehicle.

There is a large sign at the lakeside reading: DANGER. DEEP WATER NO SWIMMING, beside which a family, including two toddlers are playing in the water with a paddleboard. The dad has paddled out into the middle on his own. There is a big splash. I look up. The paddleboard is empty. He's either dived in or fallen in. There's no sign of him. Seconds pass. More seconds. Too many seconds pass. Then his head breaks the surface and he pulls himself up onto the board.

Brendan disappears for about a minute. That's all – approximately the length of time that Paddleboarding Dad was underwater. In that time, while frantically looking for him and shouting him, I'm thinking I wouldn't find him and the next thing will be I'll get a call saying he's at home and there will be a colossal taxi bill charged to my card. But then I spot him, only a matter of yards away, sitting perfectly camouflaged behind a clump of grasses. I swear he does this on purpose.

We walk a bit further around the lake, where we meet a Yorkshire couple with a lovely dog, Bella, with identical colouring to Brendan, but she's more of an Alsatian-type. Bella was a rescue dog but they'd had her since she was four months old. She's a lovely dog, good with people and she had mentored the other dogs they had fostered. She's thirteen but you wouldn't know. She doesn't sigh, moan or sit down moodily at any point. For that reason, I think Brendan is struggling to relate to her.

We chat for several minutes, during which time Brendan gets bored and slouches off like a spoilt teenager. He plonks himself down in some reeds with his tongue hanging out.

The man glances across at him and laughs. "He seems like one really cool customer. He's really chilled."

I laugh uneasily. I don't really want to say: "Oh, he's really not!" so I say nothing.

They carry on with their walk and we carry on wandering

slightly aimlessly. I'm trying to get to grips with my feelings for Ennerdale. "It's better than I expected" isn't a very comprehensive review. It certainly looks alright in the sunshine. The sun can make anywhere look nice. And the sun does keep coming out, and it goes dangerously hot, then it goes behind clouds again. We haven't had clouds for days. If it was raining here, it would change everything; it would be quite grim, oppressive, dark and barren. But when it's raining at Windermere, it's still Windermere but in the rain; there are cafes, the steamers, museums, pubs…. You're never far from amenities. When it's raining here… there's nothing really. It's raining and you get wet.

My conclusion is that I quite like Ennerdale, but Brendan *loves* it.

I've managed to find a site close by, so Brendan can reduce his travelling for the day and we can spend a lazy afternoon doing short walks and sitting on the grass relaxing. The heat becomes unbearable, despite it being overcast. The van is far too hot and airless, so we sit outside in a tiny amount of shade by the hedge. It's so hot, muggy and unpleasant. It feels like there might be thunder. It does rain briefly, but not heavily.

I go to bed around 10.30. Brendan has already been in his basket for most of the evening. I have an insomniac moment. I lie awake for hours, restless and unsettled. When I finally do sleep, I have horrific nightmares about death and destruction, blood and guts. I wake up suddenly – it's 3.30. I don't sleep again.

Lying awake for hours, I suddenly realise I can hear what

sounds like white noise; a constant background rushing noise. I think it must be my laptop. (It's not.) Or my phone. (It's not that either.) It must be the van radio then. (No.) I strain my ears to try and locate the source, then I realise, it isn't coming from inside the van. It's coming from outside. Short of an alien abduction, I can't imagine what can make a noise like that – it's all encompassing, it's everywhere, it's constant. It's a rushing... like a waterfall, like rushing water. Oh. It's water. It's the stream that runs along the side of the site. The sound has been there all along, but with traffic noises and the other daytime sounds it was easy to overlook it, to filter it out into an almost unheard background buzzing.

I lie back and listen to the sound of the stream; it's really relaxing when you actually know what it is.

* * * * * * * * * *

If Brendan Was A Human...

I don't think Human Brendan would be in a relationship. Canine Brendan has a posse of female admirers; Annie, Daisy, Willow and Evie are all in his entourage, but there are many others, including a huge number of golden retrievers. But he's quite open and honest; he never says "I'll call you." knowing full well he never will; when he tires of them he just walks off.

ABOVE: Mountain Brendan above Wastwater.

ABOVE: The imposing Great Gable and hawthorn from Wasdale Head.

ABOVE: A baking hot day at Wasdale Head. There are surprisingly few trees and we were desperate to find some shade.

ABOVE: Brendan posing on the dam at Ennerdale Water, one of his favourite lakes.

ABOVE: Brendan paddles in Ennerdale Water.

CHAPTER 6: DAYS OF WHINE AND ROSES

In which Brendan fleetingly visits the remote and secret valley of Loweswater, Crummock Water and Buttermere – only to find that it isn't even remotely secret.

It's a lovely short drive along leafy green lanes, dropping down to Loweswater. There is the occasional whitewashed cottage with roses around the door – the flowers full and starting to fall. There is soft golden sunshine and I think it's going to be hot later.

We park in a layby which is already quite busy. Brendan hops out and gazes curiously at the sky, as though trying to gauge the weather, then we set off along a footpath in the direction of the lake. Brendan seems a bit lethargic this morning and he's eating a lot of grass. He drags at first but by the time we reach a steep uphill stretch, he jogs ahead energetically. It looks like Mountain Brendan is back!

Loweswater is shimmering in the distance, across an area of marsh and marram grass. It's green and pastoral around the lake, in fact "Loweswater" means "leafy lake". It's a sleepy, bucolic area with farmed fields, sheep grazing lazily, drystone walls and fringes of trees. It's beautiful.

Brendan is in a brilliant mood, trundling along, tail high, showing a great deal of interest in his surroundings, sniffing the air, running ahead, stopping, sniffing again fervently, then inevitably cocking his leg.

For a short way we're walking adjacent to two older men, who studiously ignore us because they're too busy talking about themselves. Two approaching ladies don't even seem to notice the men, because they're intently staring at Brendan and smiling; they pass the men without a word and give us a jubilant hello, which makes our day.

We reach the lake, which is verdant, picturesque, a charming oasis, strangely out of place here, in an area that is so craggy and dramatic. It seems slightly magical and unreal. It has a backdrop of very impressive high fells, all stone and bracken. Brendan rushes to the water's edge and tentatively steps in. He saunters up and down, paddling and occasionally tasting the water. I can now reveal the water here is nice, but not as nice as Ennerdale. I sit down on a rock and I enjoy being in this beautiful place in the sunshine with my dog.

I give Brendan the choice between two treats: a sausage roll (marrowbone roll) or a cigar (chew stick). He would usually always go for the sausage roll. He sniffs them both thoughtfully, and then gently takes the cigar from my fingers. I don't know who he is anymore. This is presumably Mountain Brendan. For a few minutes he parades up and down with it sticking out of his mouth, like a business tycoon. Eventually, he lies down and holds it between his front paws and eats it.

Loweswater reminds me of Elter Water or Esthwaite Water, which are beautiful, quiet, hidden, tranquil. It is a mile long and half a mile wide – so one of the smallest lakes – and only 18 metres deep. That doesn't sound very deep, but it's still ten of me. Loweswater is unusual as it is the only lake of the sixteen that drains *inwards* – towards the centre of the Lake District – as it empties into neighbouring Crummock Water.

A rock is just breaking the surface of the water. Brendan stares at it intensely for a full two minutes. When it becomes apparent that he isn't going to win a staring competition, he suddenly starts barking at it – probably warning it off his patch. When the rock fails to respond and doesn't seem to be even slightly intimidated, I think he feels a bit foolish and tries to change the subject.

I realise I haven't had a cup of tea this morning. That can't be right! It's getting seriously hot, but I manage to find a shady layby with overhanging trees and a view over the lake. I can't believe no one else is here, it's beautiful. Brendan is able to sit in the long grass by the hedgerow and make himself a cool nest. I get my deckchair out and sit there with tea and a couple of slices of malt loaf. We're sitting in a layby, beside an almost silent road, in a rare spot of shade. This is the best thing ever. It's the type of thing my dad would do. Have I turned into him?

The leaves of the ash tree above us are falling, at a rate of one leaf every five seconds. Yes, in the interest of science I timed them. Despite the sunshine and the heat, this is still autumn.

A car pulls in and parks directly in front of us. It appears to be a set of parents with their grown-up daughter. Brendan watches them, but doesn't bark, mainly because

I don't think he can be bothered. The man says hello. He has a slight accent, but his English is so good I can't place it. The daughter starts telling them about the plants in the undergrowth. I realise they're speaking German, but I pick up the occasional English word: "blackberry" and "bramble". Then the daughter scoops up a few of the large, ripe berries and throws them into her mouth. I think: I wouldn't; they're on dog level! Then, with renowned German efficiency, they strip the layby of berries within two minutes, collecting them in a plastic box and they drive off at high speed. We're left in peace again, but with no berries.

A group of high viz cycling men appear on the roadway and stop briefly to look at the view. Still nothing from Brendan. They ask about access to the water and I give directions. As they cycle off, I hear a snatch of their conversation:

"I've only skinny-dipped once. And that was with me mate's sister."

"Oh, aye… was that before or after?"

"Before or after what?"

"*Before*… or… *after*?"

"Before or after what?"

"*Before* you did? Or *after* you did?"

"What? I don't…"

And then they're gone, so we never find out whether it

was before or after, possibly instead of – or even during. Our nomadic lives* mean we never get to hear the end of a story.

After a very leisurely break, we continue driving along the narrow, winding valley road: the only road. We park in another layby somewhere above Crummock Water and set off on foot to explore. We follow a footpath through a field of tufty grass, buttercups, thistles, clover and bracken. Brendan hears a dog barking somewhere below, so we have to stop so he can assess the situation, in case the dog needs some assistance or some advice... presumably about the best episodes of *Cash In The Attic* or something similar. The barking stops so we're allowed to continue.

We have a panoramic view of the lake below, glistening in the heat. Crummock is two-and-a-half miles long with a kink in the middle. In fact, the clue is in the name, as "crummock" means "crooked one". It is by far the largest of the three lakes in this valley; it is the undisputed boss, ruling over Loweswater to the west and Buttermere to the east. If the other two ganged up on it, they'd still lose. Crummock and Buttermere were once one large lake filling the glaciated valley. I suspect that at some point in the far distant past, again before Brendan was even born, all three had been connected.

Even though it's much less than two miles between the lakes, the setting for Crummock is so much more rugged and craggy than pretty Loweswater. The sun is so bright there is a heat haze. It's too hot for us. We seek shelter under a tree with a great view across the water. Brendan gets comfortable in the long grass and lies down for a nap. You may have gathered by now, that's what he does.

I first came here on a family holiday. We were staying in the nearby Newlands valley in a hotel. We rarely stayed in hotels, so this was quite unusual. It was rather select, as I recall, but a friend of the family worked there and Mum and Dad had got a deal. Actually, if we went anywhere it seems to have been because Mum and Dad had got a deal. That's not a criticism; I admire their frugalism and they were hard times of strikes, shortages and job uncertainty. It was mid to late autumn. It was cold and wet and foggy. Despite the weather letting us down, the Lakes made a lasting impression on me.

I remember we visited this valley. I specifically remember Crummock Water and Buttermere, standing close to the water in the cold, grey light looking at the cold, grey water. My mum would probably have been skimming stones across the glassy surface of the lake, while my dad would probably have been admiring the view. Dad loved a good view and could happily sit for hours, staring at a pleasing vista, smiling serenely. He also had a Buddhist-like temperament and would often impart great wisdom, which often began with a beatific smile and words better suited to a fridge-magnet, such as: "Well, son… you often find that's what happens in life."

Then he would lose his temper with something technical – a very expensive electric wallpaper steamer comes to mind, which failed to operate as he expected so he threw it across the garage and broke it. I'm no stranger to that myself.

I wonder if Brendan takes after his parents. Of course, he never knew his father and his mother was a dubious character; he's very private about his secret past, so we'll never know.

After a suitable time of relaxation for Brendan, we step out from the shade of the oak tree into the glare of the sun; it's unpleasantly, scarily hot now.

We set off driving towards Buttermere. Yet again there are cars everywhere. Every legitimate car park and parking space is filled, with lines of vehicles waiting for a space. But also, every verge and every gateway has a car rammed in it, almost completely blocking the road. There are tailbacks because drivers are having to manoeuvre slowly around abandoned vehicles. It's so stressful.

The road draws alongside Buttermere, which looks absolutely beautiful; the lighting is just right. Between the road and the water is a fringe of woodland, the water itself looks iridescent and the fells opposite make a spectacular backdrop. I'm quite shocked just how stunningly beautiful it is. I'm desperate to stop and walk along its shore, though I know Brendan is desperate not to stop and not to walk along any part of it or anywhere. He wins, because we can't stop. We literally can't stop. There isn't a parking space to be had anywhere in the valley. Every available space is taken. There's nowhere to stop, nowhere to pull in, nowhere to wait. And then we're leaving Buttermere behind. That was it. Gone.

We're suddenly in a steep-sided valley and the road is starting to climb. The valley is rugged, sheer, oppressive even; the sides are so high it's quite dizzying. Once we're too far away to walk back to the lake, there are indeed parking spaces. I pull over in an empty spot and we go for a walk down to the stream in the base of the treeless valley, so we can paddle. Brendan has a good drink and dips his paws before sitting down. With no shade at all available, it's much too hot to stay long. We have to return to the van, where Brendan lies down in the narrow strip of shade cast by the bonnet.

I sit in my deckchair under the awning, looking back along the dale towards the shining jewel that is Buttermere. Tom Cruise recently parachuted in for a scene in Mission: Impossible, Dead Reckoning. They say his character is based loosely on Brendan Freedog. I don't know how true that is. It was Brendan who told me, in confidence.

It has really annoyed me that we've missed out on beautiful Buttermere. I'm agitated and not happy about it, so we try walking back, but after ten minutes Brendan is severely dragging and it's too hot and just too far.

There is a scraping from above and two jets pass low overhead. A moment later, five helicopters come from the opposite direction, flying in formation towards the sea. I've never seen that many airborne helicopters in my life. It's quite a sight as they pass low over the lake. I half expect to see Tom Cruise parachuting down. Perhaps he does it due to the lack of parking. I wish we'd thought of it.

We return to the van and set off up the steepening road towards the pass. There is a warning sign: maximum width is 6.6. We just qualify. The landscape suddenly changes; it's gone from lush near the lake, to rugged grassy moorland, and then it changes again and suddenly it's naked rock, strewn boulders everywhere, steep scree. It's a harsh, unforgiving landscape. You wouldn't want to break down here in the winter. You probably wouldn't want to break down here at all, regardless of the season. The road winds ahead, steeply rising and very narrow. The engine is screaming and we're in first gear. It's now shady and quite cold, because of the high sides to the valley. It's like another world: barren, alien.

We follow the tightly twisting road to the Honister Pass at the top. At the summit is the Honister Slate Mine, which quarries and works Westmorland green slate. Next to the slate works is Honister Hause Youth Hostel. I stayed here on a school walking holiday. I would have been about thirteen, I suppose. We walked from Elterwater. I can't remember the route but it was a very long way.

Somewhere towards the end of that walk, I somehow managed to collide with a triangular road sign and the sharp edge of it went into my forehead. I can't believe I didn't have a deep gash, but as far as I know there was no mark. However, I did feel sick and ill for the next 24 hours. I now realise I had concussion, but at the time I was just busy trying to behave normally. Normally-ish. I didn't want to draw attention to myself and I didn't want people to know I had collided with a road sign. Everyone was watching where they were putting their feet and I don't think anyone noticed what had happened, but one of the boys did ask what the very audible clang was – my head striking the sign. This school trip further fuelled my love of walking and the countryside – and in particular the Lake District.

The Honister summit is quite bleak, but as we drive ahead the view becomes alpine, like southern Europe, like some of the mountain scenes in *The Persuaders* again. Now we're out of the pass, it's hot once more and there are sun-baked rocks and spindly fir trees. It's stunning.

We drop down into the green valley of Borrowdale, where Nicky has booked us a campsite as we've had no signal all day. I turn into a camping field, but I'm not sure it's the right place. The instant I pull on the handbrake, there's a ruddy-faced man at the window.

"Yes, hello, what can I do for you?"

"Is this Stonethwaite?"

"No… what d'you want to go there for?"

"The campsite."

"What for? Are you going to a rave? Because that's what'll be going on tonight!" He starts laughing and carries on laughing for some time.

I'm not sharing the joke. I can't believe Brendan isn't barking at him, but there's not a word from him in the back.

He suddenly stops laughing. "No, you need to turn right, right again, left, right, along the road and right. But you'd be better off here. No one wants a rave."

"Yes, but it's booked, so I feel I've got to…"

"Whatever." He shrugs and then laughs again. "Enjoy

your rave."

As I'm leaving, with a very heavy heart, I notice a sign at the gate and I realise this is the correct site. I park and walk over to him. He starts laughing again.

"Did I put you off?"

I tell him this is where I'm supposed to be. I tell him my partner booked via the phone. He shrugs again. He has no idea. It's not a booking sort of place; he's not a booking sort of man. He tells me to go where I want. The main field is quite busy, but there is an additional field over the road. "The Quiet Field" he calls it. Obviously, we choose that. There are just a couple of other vans. We go to the opposite end of the field to them and pull up. Awning out, chair out, dog out.

This is the life. Brendan stretches out in the grass in the shade cast by the van. I sit with a can of Guinness enjoying the stunning views of Borrowdale. We're cradled in the lush valley, surrounded by tree-covered rocky fells. It's leafy and unspoilt and breath-takingly beautiful. Again, sitting here with my dog on a beautiful sunny afternoon is blissful.

We sit out for a while, so Brendan can have a long rest after his drive here, then as it's a Friday night like any young bucks* we walk across the fields to the pub, which is a mile away. It's a pleasant walk and it's sunny but less hot. The pub isn't great. It's functional and uninspiring. A proper writer might have engaged the locals and wrung out some local colour. However, there aren't any locals, all the staff are from eastern Europe. The customers aren't local either; they're all tourists, walkers, trippers. No one is speaking.

* I know... but we went anyway.

I have a pint of Guinness – alcohol free – and I allow Brendan to choose where we sit. I've trained him well, because he goes to the furthest table in a corner, dives underneath and stretches out on the cool tiled floor. I don't hear from him again. I'm the weirdo in the corner with the weird dog. After a sudden flurry at the bar has died down, there are only three grey-bearded solo drinkers remaining, all sitting alone, all nursing a pint, all reading and very glad to be alone in a pub with a book. Brendan is the only dog and the only one not reading. We're all very comfortable being alone. And we're all weirdos. Especially Brendan – but he's *my* weirdo.

When we get back to the site, the "Quiet Field" – as the owner had sold it to us – is not even remotely quiet and barely resembles a field. It's one vast, over-crowded trailer park. Every five minutes the laughing owner speeds past in his silver truck and installs someone else, wedging them in between existing tents and vans. He keeps telling people "Go where you want. Anywhere's fine. There's a space there..." There really isn't. "Or you could go between those two..." You really couldn't. "Anywhere. Go anywhere. Go where you want." And where people want to go, seemingly, is the maximum distance from us.

The rest of the site is so tightly packed, it is surely in breach of countless fire regulations; there are vans, tents, and the new car-tents. I've never seen a car tent before;

it's a case on the roof rack which opens up to form a tent on top of the car. They look really odd, incongruous and unstable, but they seem to be very popular. All these vehicles and tents are jammed-in together, and then there's us, alone on our side of the field; our van is an island and there is a sea of green surrounding us. I don't know whether it's me that's intimidating people: six-foot-four of scowling loveliness, or Brendan: less than six-foot-four, but with similar scowling loveliness and a growl thrown in for good measure. I don't know what it is, but it's working and I wish I could bottle it.

After we've gone to bed, we still hear the owner driving in with yet more people to wedge in. Brendan is breathing steadily in his basket. I check my phone, but already know there is no signal. It feels very wrong not being able to say goodnight to Nicky.

* * * * * * * * * *

If Brendan Was A Human…

People might think Human Brendan is moody, aloof and introverted – probably because he's being moody, aloof and introverted, because Canine Brendan is also moody, aloof and introverted.

ABOVE & BELOW: Beautiful Loweswater – "the leafy lake".

ABOVE & BELOW: Our van: the bliss of solitude.

ABOVE: Brendan relaxes... for a change.

CHAPTER 7: UP NORTH

In which Brendan dips his toes in the northern lakes of Derwentwater, Bassenthwaite Lake and Thirlmere – and the weather finally breaks.

I slept very well and didn't wake up until 6am. That's almost unheard of for me. Brendan has also slept very well, but that's completely normal for him.

It's surprisingly cold. When I open the curtains, I see a thick, swirling mist smothering all the other tents. That's my kind of mist! A new tent has been set up on our side of the field. They must have assembled it in the night, but I didn't hear them. They were either incredibly quiet or I was in a very deep sleep. Brendan didn't bark at them either, but that doesn't mean he didn't hear them; he can be quite intermittent with his barking, depending on how tired he is. If anyone ever breaks in to murder us and Brendan's feeling lethargic, we're done for.

By 7am the site is alive with movement. This is another location for proper walkers. People are dressed and heading for a big day out on the fells. But not Brendan. Unfortunately, I accidentally drop the tea towel on his head while brewing up. He looks up slowly – he's not impressed. The tea towel is still in place and he looks uncannily like Mother Theresa. He doesn't say anything, but I suspect he's compiling a grudge list. With a sigh, he lowers his head, curls up and goes back to sleep, still sporting the tea towel.

I sit and eat my breakfast, looking out at the mass exodus from the site. Most people are very well-equipped walking types with all The Gear. In my trainers and non-designer clothing, I don't fit in, and my high maintenance dog doesn't fit in either, though he is expertly accessorized with a tea towel. Perhaps that's the reason people are so reluctant to communicate with us. It's just my latest theory. I remove the tea towel from Brendan's head and encourage him to get up. The caustic look he gives me proves he's definitely nothing like Mother Theresa.

* * * * * * * * * *

We arrive at the jewel of Borrowdale, the Bowder Stone. We park in a small layby and then walk through attractive woodland to reach the stone itself. Yes, it's basically a big stone. A rock. Quite a big rock. It's a huge andesite lava boulder which fell 200 metres from the crag above and came to rest here. Considering it's been in situ for at least 10,000 years, it still looks incongruous. It doesn't look like an outcrop of rock; it looks like a huge marble that's rolled here and come to rest. It's over 9 metres high and 15 metres across. It is estimated to weigh over 200 metric tonnes, so it won't be rolling off any time soon. Hopefully.

Perhaps the main thing that makes this into a tourist attraction – rather than just a big rock – is the ladder staircase that leads to the top. The Victorians liked to come here on their tour of the Lakes and perambulate about and take some tea. There is still a stairway, now an elegant design in wrought iron. I'm sure it used to be wooden.

This is another place with strong memories for me. Mum and Dad brought us here on that first childhood holiday to the Lakes; they were very fond of free activities. It was another fairly damp and dismal day weatherwise, but we excitedly climbed the stairs to the top of the stone. It's funny, in my memory it appears much larger.

The current metal stairs aren't really Brendan-friendly. I take a few steps up and ask him if he's going to come with me. He looks up to the top and then sits down. I take that as a no. I tell him to wait there and not wander off. I'm as surprised as anyone when he actually does as I've asked. He watches me as I rise up the beautiful steps. I go as quickly as possible, in case someone appears along the footpath and Brendan eats them. At the top there is just a viewing station really and the view is fairly similar to the view from the ground, but a bit higher. I lean over and wave at Brendan. He looks nonplussed, but that's his way of showing affection and excitement – as well as boredom and irritation.

I hurry down as I can hear voices through the trees: a tour party of Americans led by a bearded, long-haired tour guide called Rabbie. Brendan has relocated to a rock and is sitting posing for all he's worth.

"Look at that!" Rabbie stops; his party all duly stop. He's looking at Brendan, but from a safe distance. "That's such a photo opportunity!"

"It's basically his way of getting an extra sit down." I say.

"Brilliant!"

I get my phone primed to capture the moment and Brendan – as usual – goes very self-conscious and keeps looking away. There are so many perfect photographic moments which have been ruined because of his coyness.

"He's a stunning dog!" Rabbie says.

The tour party mumble politely, but I get the impression the general feeling is: "We haven't paid good money to come and look at a dog! We have those in the States."

"He's gorgeous!" Rabbie enthuses, but still wisely keeps his distance. "What a striking animal!"

"He's yours for a pound." I say.

"Done!" he says with enthusiasm, but then immediately disappears.

I can hear Rabbie on the other side of the stone and I learn a lot from him, but don't pay him a cent. For example, the Bowder Stone claims to be the largest boulder in the world. But then Brendan makes a lot of similar claims and I seldom believe him.

We set off back through the woods towards the van. This has been a very nice little trip down Memory Lane. I also came with Nicky and our dog Cindy, probably 30 years ago. We came to the Lakes a lot. And then we stopped coming and I'm not too sure why.

Brendan stops and sniffs a tree stump. He knows I always let him stop and sniff, because sniffing (and weeing) are an important part of being a dog. It's like catching up on local news. However, sometimes – like now – it's just a delaying tactic, because he's stopped sniffing and he's having a break, just staring into space vacantly.

"Er… hello?" I say.

He immediately starts sniffing again with absolute conviction, but it's false, I wasn't born yesterday, so we move on.

Brendan's laziness never ceases to amaze me. When I first got him, I thought he must be in pain or there was something wrong with him, so I took him to the vets. After some poking and prodding and some inevitable barking, the conclusion was: he's just lazy. Some dogs are, apparently, "just lazy".

I've passed about a dozen people this morning and every single one has said hello or good morning. Maybe the curse has been lifted.

We drive through Borrowdale and come to the impressive Lodore Falls, tumbling 100 feet down a cleft in the rocks. Beside it stands the Lodore Falls Hotel, the grey bulk dwarfed by the tree-covered fells that rise steeply behind it. It was built in 1870 and has a distinct Victorian austerity about it. It has a tower and is rather gothic and sinister, a great place for a horror movie or as the setting for the hotel in *The Shining*. This isn't a criticism, to me anything gothic and atmospheric is a plus point. It is now a modern luxury spa. I could see Brendan enjoying a seaweed wrap, a deep tissue massage and a pawdicure, so I actually check out the prices – and that's why we drive on.

The road draws alongside Derwentwater, the third largest lake and surely one of – if not *the* – most beautiful. It's just under three miles long and it has many islands, one of which is inhabited. Like Windermere, it has a ferry service around the lake, which I've used many times in the past. Cruising around this stunning lake by boat is the perfect way to spend a day. Of course, that's top of Brendan's list of things not to do. It's just a guess, but I imagine he's scheduling a sit down somewhere.

There are various small parking places along the shore, but they are all full. It's Buttermere all over again. I inch my way through several of them, but they're completely packed. Why isn't everyone back at school and work or on remand? I suddenly realise my mistake. When travelling, days tend to lose their significance. Not that I always know what the day is, even when at home, but today is – apparently – a Saturday. It's the weekend and I have unwittingly brought us into one of the tourist hotspots, Keswick, at the busiest time.

It's too late to change plans, we're committed and we're coming into Keswick now, a handsome market town and tourist destination at the top of Derwentwater. I try to get Brendan enthused about one of the local attractions – the Pencil Museum.

"It's a museum – *of pencils*!" You can't come to Keswick without visiting. "After all, who doesn't love a pencil?" Apparently, Brendan. As I'd suspected, he has indeed made alternate plans and intends to have a sit down instead, and this will include no items of stationery. Though he will be stationary for the duration.

It's a slow drag through the town centre: traffic, traffic lights, people, seagulls. Keswick was famously the home of Lake Poets Robert Southey and Samuel Taylor Coleridge. They didn't have to put up with this sort of traffic! Life moved at a slower pace then; it moved more at Brendan's pace – and in so many ways I wish it would now. I jam my hand on the horn and start remonstrating at the driver in the next vehicle. I don't, but that would be so poetic.

As a magnificent backdrop to the town, above the slate roofs and chimneypots is the massive bulk of its attendant fell, Skiddaw, a huge rambling green beast. Everest mountaineer Sir Chris Bonington lives in a village on the far side. I read that he climbed the fell every morning before his Frosties, to keep fit. I saw him once; I smiled in recognition and he smiled back, but I didn't speak to him. I have only climbed Skiddaw once, but it's once more than Brendan.

I follow the car park signs and eventually we pull into the large lakeside car park, where there are surprisingly lots of spaces. Trying to get a parking ticket is like an initiation test. And I fail. Repeatedly. The machine is so complicated. I abort three times and let the person behind get their ticket, whilst I watch them closely, then try to replicate what they did. In the end, a piece of paper comes out so I put it in the window and hope it will suffice. I'm really stressed now and need to do something to unwind. The Pencil Museum? Apparently not an option. A lake cruise? Vetoed. So a walk then – a short walk – a really short walk followed by a lengthy sit down? We've hit the jackpot.

I slide open the side door and Brendan sleepily hops out. "Oh great... another car park." He can't think of anywhere he'd less like to be. Except the Pencil Museum. Or on a boat.

We follow the crowds along the road towards the lake. It's busy. Too busy. Hot and sticky and overcrowded. We come into sight of Derwentwater, which opens up and lets the sky in, with the most eye-catching fells surrounding it. It looks like some sort of pre-Raphaelite painting. I don't really know what that means, but it's definitely what it looks like. I feel this could be Greece or Italy. And this time I'm talking about a historical setting, rather than a location shoot for *The Persuaders*. Bizarrely, Derwentwater was used as a planet in Star Wars: The Force Awakens, though with quite a bit of CGI added.

The views are breath-taking: shining blue water, blue skies, dramatic fells rich in the tints of autumn. It's almost impossible to take it in. At this moment I think Derwentwater is the most beautiful lake. No wonder it's so popular. Apparently, it smells great for dogs as well, because Brendan's nose is working overtime and the walk takes about eight times longer than it should. It's also packed out with dogs of every make and model, so there's plenty of greeting, sniffing and growling and from Brendan a fair amount of snubbing; he's in his element.

We manage to get onto the shingle beach and escape the crowd. Brendan scampers to the water and daintily dips his front paws in. He is about to take a drink, but he hesitates, has a sniff and then backs away. It looks like Derwentwater fails his test. There are probably too many boats at this point and the water is less clean. He's very disappointed.

We return to the busy footpath. We – and everyone else – are walking to Friar's Crag, a well-known beauty spot. It's a lovely shady, tree-lined walk, but it's so busy that it's not really like a peaceful lakeside stroll, it's more like walking to a football match on a Saturday afternoon. People are shuffling along; it's too tightly packed to overtake. It's actually quite claustrophobic. Brendan is doing surprisingly well, probably because of all the sensory input. That's the smell of dog wee to you and me.

Amongst the trees, facing the lake is a monolithic memorial to John Ruskin (1819-1900), the artist, critic, philanthropist and environmentalist: any one of those most people would love to have on their CV. Ruskin was all of these and so much more. Today he would probably be equivalent to a social media influencer. But he wasn't, he isn't and he probably never would be. The stone is from Borrowdale and features a sculpture in bronze of Ruskin's profile, a chiselled religious quotation and a passage from Ruskin himself: "The first thing I remember, as an event in life, was being taken by my nurse to the brow of Friar's Crag on Derwent Water."

My earliest memory is of my mum getting some socks out of a drawer for me. Admittedly, Ruskin's memory is the more evocative and poetic, and looks better carved into stone than my sock memory would.

While Brendan sniffs a conifer, I turn my attention to the view. Again, I can't really take it in. It's so astoundingly beautiful; the water, the boats, the islands, the classical outline of the low fells opposite, the woodland on the far shore, the clouds, the pine-scented air. Ruskin once described this view as "one of the three most beautiful scenes in Europe." I don't think he's far wrong, but it begs the question: Where are the two places which are even more beautiful?

We continue with the crowds. It's too busy, but we go through a gate off the main path and find a strangely quiet parkland area with benches overlooking the lake. It's now dangerously hot in the direct sun and there's no shade, so we can't stay long. I sit on a bench, enjoying the view over the lake. Instead of sitting on the soft grass, Brendan parks himself in the middle of the stony pathway. A Korean couple come along and stop. The man looks at Brendan and laughs. He has an SLR camera with a massive telephoto lens, which he points at my dog and starts taking photographs of him.

I call Brendan to me, to get him out of the way. He glances at me then looks away.

"Don't ignore me! You're blocking the path! Come out of the way!"

The man laughs heartily. "He understand what you say?"

"He understands every word. But he chooses not to do anything about it."

He laughs again. "So funny!"

His wife says something to me in Korean – my Korean is quite rusty – but she's holding up her own camera – a junior version of her husband's with a standard lens.

She points repeatedly at Brendan and then her camera. I smile and nod, assuming she wants to take a photograph. And she does, but she goes right up to him and thrusts the camera in his face. Brendan was never going to accept this. Never. And neither would I. Brendan barks at her, but he remains lying down, so he's basically issuing a simple warning. The woman leaps back with a squeal, but then immediately leans forward again and jams the camera in his personal space. Brendan barks again. She leaps back again. This goes on repeatedly. Barking, screaming, repeat. The husband is laughing. The wife is nervous but seems determined to get the picture she wants and Brendan is adamant that she isn't. Brendan is getting agitated, so I slip him on his lead and drag him away, grumbling.

We find a way onto the shore and sit for a long time in the slim shade of a solitary pine tree. Within minutes there are people sitting all around us. It's like Woodstock, except it's not 1969 and no one is wearing flares. Neither of us like crowds of people. If there are more than about three people at Brendan's field at home, we feel uneasy.

A Japanese family station themselves right next to us, far too close. If he wasn't feeling so lethargic Brendan would have something to say about it. We are about to be adopted as part of their extended family, so we make a move and head back along the tree-lined path towards the town with the ambling crowds. In front of us is a father and very small girl. We witness democracy in action.

The dad asks her: "Can I have a mucky beer this afternoon?"

The girl is little more than a toddler, but incredibly articulate and well-spoken. "Yes. But later on. Not now."

"So what shall we do now?"

"I suggest we go into a coffee shop." the child says.

"And what time shall we go to the playground?"

"Two o'clock."

She must be a savant. Either that or she's his wife and she's in her thirties but has a chromosome disorder. They disappear amongst the moving people and we turn off into Crow Park – famous for crows. (This is just a guess.) It's an open green area with views along almost the entirety of the lake. There are lots of people having picnics or paddling. Again, it looks like a painting – not that I know very much about art and I'm no artist; I can't even crayon within the lines.

There's no shade at all in the park, so Brendan very kindly sits behind me to use me as a human shade-provider. He gets himself comfortable and has a nap. I look out over the lake. The views from here are amazing. The relatively small, but distinctive fell, Cat Bells, in particular, draws the eye. I've climbed this many times with Nicky and our dog, Cindy. I'm obviously not going to be climbing it with Brendan. At the end of the lake, looking far away and mysterious are the distinctive "Jaws of Borrowdale", the interlocking spurs of the valley, where we stayed last night.

The lake itself is alive with launches, rowing boats

and paddleboarders. Like Windermere, it looks very lively and cosmopolitan. If Windermere is the ocean, Derwentwater is an inland sea. It is much more contained than Windermere, compact, almost round, whereas Windermere is long and sinuous.

I came here several times with my parents, in their large motorhome, and we stayed on a site at the head of the lake, with a very similar view to this. Mum and Dad were never big walkers. They were of the familiar breed of motorhomers who would sit on a deckchair outside their van – something I am doing increasingly these days, but it's mainly down to Brendan. My Mum would more than likely be pondering over a crossword, whilst Dad would be smiling serenely and looking at the view and also saying hello to everyone who passed, until people got the measure of him and stopped passing.

I've also been here many times with Nicky. We even camped in the hills overlooking the lake, in the days before she unilaterally banned all camping activity. It's quite odd to think she ever agreed to it in the first place. Mind you, I wouldn't do it now either and I know Brendan seconds that.

I really love Derwentwater. It's visually stunning. I don't think you can stand on its shore and not get an amazing view. It has a majesty, a grandeur. It's timeless. It's a living postcard. But it's very popular, it's very busy and it's weekend. It's also very hot. We can't stay long in this blazing heat and the number of people here are suffocating the splendour of the landscape.

* * * * * * * * *

In the afternoon – partly to escape the thronging masses – we visit Thirlmere. We park in a layby off the main road. A footpath leads through woodland to a viewpoint over the lake. Mountain Brendan is scampering excitedly through the pine trees, occasionally waiting for me to catch up. He's energised after his long rest this afternoon and impatient to get on with the walk, racing ahead through the bracken, then waiting, watching me, tongue out, then darting ahead again. I love watching Mountain Brendan.

The path leads to a small rocky plateau. By the time I climb up, Brendan has already found himself a comfortable hollow in the stone and is reclining in a leisurely fashion. I sit next to him and gaze out at the view over the lake, far below, at the deep water.

I used to think Thirlmere was quite severe, quite dark, and looked like a stark, clinical, man-made reservoir surrounded by never-changing pine forests. I think over the decades the Forestry Commission has done a good job of softening the surrounding landscape, mixing the trees, so they contain some native broadleaves, so it looks quite natural and colourful.

So, this is Thirlmere – home of great water. That's not a review, I'm just quoting what the sign says. I can't really comment on the water's greatness for myself, though this is where the majority of my drinking water comes from, as the Thirlmere reservoir was created by the Manchester Corporation to supply water to the growing city. Manchester was the birthplace of the Industrial Revolution, though I didn't take part in it myself, you understand. The city needed vast amounts of water for its industries and its workers and after exhausting local supplies, they looked to the Lake District.

The reservoir opened in 1894. Water is transported from here to my tap, travelling 95 miles along an aqueduct. It takes around a day for the water to arrive in Manchester, so when I turn on my tap at home, I'm getting water from Thirlmere that started its journey yesterday. The reservoir provides up to 227 litres per day, though I only use a fraction of that, and Brendan even less, as he hardly ever drinks anything.

The Thirlmere aqueduct is the longest gravity-fed aqueduct in the country, meaning that the water moves downhill with no need for any pumps along the entirety of its length. It ends in Heaton Park reservoir, Manchester, where it joins water from other sources and is then piped directly into my home – and probably the homes of others. It's quite an amazing feat.

But apart from the thirsty cotton-weaving Mancs, not everyone was thrilled by the proposed scheme. Originally, there was a small hour-glass-shaped natural lake in the bottom of this valley, surrounded by a few farmsteads and cottages. The building of the dam would mean these would all be flooded and the valley would be changed forever. There was a small, organised opposition from John Ruskin, amongst other notables of the day. After many years they lost the campaign, the dam was built, the houses in the valley were demolished and the waters rose.

Though the campaign failed, it was a hugely important failure and led to many successes. This is now considered to be the first environmental action and has been scrutinised all over the world. Some proponents went on to form what became the National Trust, which has had a powerful impact on the landscape. As failures go – with hindsight – the Thirlmere campaign was a great success.

Today's Thirlmere is just under four miles long with a maximum depth of 40 metres. While it looks very comfortable and natural in its valley, I feel it has no heart. It has no community as such. It is disenfranchised. The reservoir is on the busy route between Ambleside and Keswick, which links the central and the northern lakes, so it is seen by thousands of people every day who speed past in their cars but don't stop. And I think that sums up my relationship with Thirlmere; I have usually been on that road heading elsewhere and I have seldom stopped. I *have* been here on occasion, of course, mainly with Nicky, but usually I've driven past and not given Thirlmere a second glance, because it isn't Derwentwater and it isn't Windermere. It's the lonely, dark reservoir in-between that provides my water.

This trip is all about reassessing what I know or think I know. Right now, Thirlmere looks beautiful and we're in a nice, quiet spot, no one else is around and we have an unspoilt view over the water. Everything is very calm and peaceful, then Brendan suddenly starts barking. In the opposite direction, away from the lake, he can see two tiny people coming down from Helvellyn. This could go on for quite a while. I sit in front of him, blocking his view of the walkers. He stops barking and sits calmly for a moment, then realises what I've done, so he cranes his neck to peer around me and starts barking again. This continues until the two people thankfully drop below the treeline. He immediately stops barking and sits there quite at peace.

There is a very welcome cool breeze. The pines around us stir, their boughs creek. Everything is very tranquil. I could stay here on this little plateau indefinitely, but soon after five o'clock it starts to rain; only a few drops at first and I decide we'll sit it out. Brendan decides we won't sit it out. He stands up and is itching to get going. It turns out he's right – within a few minutes it's really thrashing down. The lake below looks very dramatic, storm-torn. Brendan sets off through the trees and I follow. He instinctively knows the shortest way back to the car park. He has an unfailing sense of direction. He's like a flawless homing pigeon; the kind of homing pigeon that likes watching daytime TV and napping.

We get back to the van and have a drive around the lake in the rain. The Thirlmere dam road is closed, has been closed for a couple of years and will possibly remain closed due to trees unearthed in a storm and rocks falling onto the road. There is a strong protest group calling for the reopening of the road, so Thirlmere is once again the scene of protest. But we won't be stopped, as there are other ways around the reservoir.

The quiet western road is tree-lined and very pleasant, even in the rain. I remember coming here with my mum and dad, in their van, stopping off in a layby for a cup of tea. I had wanted to go in a café in Keswick, but they said "What's the point, there's no need. We can have a brew in the van and it won't cost a penny." I argued that it's as much about the experience as anything. It's funny, I'd be much more inclined to stay in my van now, especially with Brendan.

So we had a brew in the van. Dad always had tea, mum always had coffee. And that sums them up really, complete opposites. I have tea and coffee and like them equally in different ways. We did a daily crossword together, which – as they grew older – was something they loved doing. Dad would read the clues and excitedly shout out the first thing that came into his head. Mum would allow a suitable pause and then provide the correct answer. At the end, after Dad had written in all the answers Mum had provided, he'd fold the newspaper and say: "Well, that's another one I've done for you." Which is something I say to this day. I see myself in both my parents, though I never wear a flat cap.

When we've completed our circuit of Thirlmere it's still raining quite heavily, the sun has gone completely and it is several degrees cooler. This is perfect! I have to go shopping for essential provisions – especially food for Brendan – and I didn't know how I was going to do this, because I couldn't leave him in the van in the heat, but now it won't be a problem. I drive into Keswick and leave Brendan resting in his basket with all the curtains closed. I run into the small supermarket and grab a trolley.

It's very stressful going shopping and I always feel panicked leaving Brendan, even though he's only a few yards away, it's broad daylight and the car park is busy. I run up and down the aisles and hurl things into a trolley. If I can't find something immediately, I delete it from the list. I pay and charge back out to the van. When I open the side door, Brendan looks up quizzically from his basket. I don't think he'd even noticed I'd gone.

As it's the weekend and very busy, we were lucky to find a campsite at all, but we had to settle for one some distance away. It's also busy, but they fit us in. We're put in another large, open-plan free-for-all tent field. I park in the only available space and let Brendan out. It's cool but has stopped raining. He stretches out in the long grass. I sit in my deckchair and crack open a newly procured Guinness.

The views of the surrounding countryside are very nice, but the site is too full, and we're right next to the path and gate leading to the toilet block, so we get a lot of foot traffic. Brendan barks at first, then gives up, thankfully. As I'm sitting here, I start to realise why this was the only vacant space on the site. We're right next to the septic tanks, so it absolutely stinks. As the evening wears on, the toilets get quite a hammering and the stench gets worse and worse.

Our nearest neighbours are what appears to be a leather-clad motorbike couple with long hair, tattoos, piercings and heavy metal T-shirts, but they don't have a motorbike – they have a sensible Volvo estate in a conservative dark burgundy colour. They also have several children to fill it with. Unlike some previous sites, there is no noise from them and they seem very well-behaved. Instead, the parents are constantly interacting with them; they talk to them all night and engage with them fully. They don't once send them to play on the other side of the site and annoy other people instead.

After he's had his tea, I take Brendan for a walk along the adjacent lane. We meet a nice older man with a working collie. "He's a failed farm dog." he tells me. "He's traumatised. They treat them like objects, don't they? I basically rescued him. The farmer said take him if you want, just don't bring him back. So, I did. He's scared of everything... brushes..."

"Oh, so's he." I say, looking at Brendan. "And leaf blowers..."

"Metal food bowls..."

"Crockery..."

"Cupboards..."

"Bins..."

"Moving vehicles..."

"Stationary vehicles..."

"Planes..."

"The hoover!" I say, "That causes a real issue... So I can't hoover as often as I should."

He smiles. "Oh, no. What a terrible shame."

We chat for ages. Our respective dogs, both on their leads, sit a few feet apart, back-to-back, both ignoring each other, both ignoring us as we discuss them at length. He's such a friendly man; it's very refreshing at a time when my current opinion of people is very low. It's like a trip back in time to when people were less rude.

It seems that everyone else on the site with a dog is queueing up to talk to the friendly man and we've had our turn so we move on.

Brendan has a relaxing evening doing what he does best: nothing. The light fades, the sky goes black, but is peppered with pinpoint stars. There is very little light pollution so we have an unspoilt view of the heavens. I can see all the classic constellations, the Plough, Orion, Cassiopeia. I can hear Rocker Dad next door answering questions about the universe.

"Well, each one of the stars is a sun, like our sun." He hasn't once stopped engaging with them. "And many of them have got their own solar systems… planets circling them… like ours."

They appear to have two girls and a boy. Tomorrow they are planning a single gender evening. The girls have chosen to do a pamper session with the mum: face packs and painting their nails. Rocker Dad suggests he and Rock Boy have a gaming session. The boy excitedly agrees. It's heart-warming to see parents enjoying quality time with their children.

We're both in bed by 9.30. I'm so tired and of course, Brendan is always tired; he excels at being tired. Unfortunately, he needs to go out for a wee in the small hours. It's freezing cold. The stars look even more amazing, because the campsite is now completely dark and completely silent. Standing there looking upwards, I can see the Milky Way, sprinkled across the sky like icing sugar. It's an incredible sight. But Brendan's had enough now, so stargazing is cut short.

We return to the van and he hops into his basket and is

fast asleep before I've even closed the sliding door.

* * * * * * * * * *

We awake early – or rather we're awoken – to a crashing sound like metal scraping along concrete. I can't see anything outside, but it's done the job: we're both wide awake. Brendan raises his head, looks at me, decides whatever the noise is, I can deal with it and he flops down again.

The cacophony has stopped: I never find out what it was. It's 6.06. I'm still very tired. It's a misty start, then the sun comes out. It's a Sunday. I think. But it may well not be.

We drive away from the site before 8.30; I'm glad to get away. We park at Dodd Wood, on the eastern shore of Bassenthwaite Lake, the only one of the sixteen lakes actually called "lake" rather than mere or water. It is the fourth largest lake at four miles long. I catch glimpses of it; it looks beautiful and is surrounded by lush green countryside.

We set off along a waymarked trail leading uphill through the conifer forest. Brendan is very sluggish at present. He can't really be bothered; morning is his most energetic time, so it's not looking good for the rest of the day.

Apart from re-acquainting myself with the Lakes and introducing them to Brendan, I was hoping this trip would revitalise us. Apart from the fact that right at this moment Brendan looks bleary-eyed, half asleep and hung-over, I think he's generally doing better than me at the whole revitalising thing. We're doing more exercise than normal, we're walking further and we're doing some steep gradients, so we're using different muscles, but it's not helping me sleep. Most nights my sleep has been terrible.

Once we've been walking for a few minutes I notice Mountain Brendan is back, skipping ahead merrily and stopping every so often to sniff and wee, and it's me who's wondering if there's a taxi service or a convenient stair lift. But I'm very happy to be here. It's a bit cooler today and I've put a jacket on for the first time in ages. Although we're encased in a conifer forest, the strip of sky above is pale blue and the birds are singing.

We're following a red waymarked trail. I picked the red one because it was the shortest – I was thinking of Brendan, honestly – and I thought it would be the easiest. Clearly, I was wrong.

A boy in his early teens overtakes us, playing music out loud. It sounds like Bollywood or something similar. He's walking really fast and doing a sort of dancing, flailing his arms and waving his hands around, so it probably is Bollywood music and this is Bollywood dancing. I say hello to him, but he doesn't reply; he just passes us by. I don't think he even sees us; he's lost in music – caught in a trap. Brendan doesn't bark at him. The boy disappears uphill into the distance and he's gone.

We carry on. It was only a year ago that we walked up Holyhead Mountain; we seemed to do it with such ease. Of course, I was a year younger then; Brendan was *seven* years younger. Mountain Brendan seems to be failing slightly now. His tongue is lolling out and his footsteps are heavy. I suspect I look the same.

We reach a junction of paths. The red route continues uphill, while there is a short cut, a blue route, which leads downhill, back to the car park. I decide we've probably done the majority of the uphill stretches now and the rest should be much easier, so I carry on ahead. Brendan stands his ground and keeps looking between me and the signpost. How can he know this? He has an amazing sense of direction. He would make an excellent Mountain Rescue dog, though his laziness would let him down; he'd take one look at the mountains and then retreat to his fireside and plasma screen.

We're at an impasse. Brendan's eyes are wide and his mouth open; he can't believe we're not bailing and taking the easy route. Neither can I really. I call him, but he stands fast. Mountain Brendan has definitely bailed. In the end I have to temporarily put his lead on and guide him away, assuring him it will be easier. And I'm wrong. Again. There's a lot more uphill yet.

Next, he tries SniffTactics ©Brendan Freedog. He starts sniffing every blade of grass in turn, every dandelion, every tree, every twig. He's putting a lot of effort in; his face-acting is award winning. He's so expressive. It's like a beautiful canine mime; no words are needed. He's seemingly absolutely engrossed by the smells around here and is very busy. Unfortunately for him, he keeps glancing at me to make sure I'm clocking his display, which gives away that it's all a delaying tactic. We carry on uphill, whether he likes it or not, but it's not easy-going. Thankfully, we meet two very nice ladies with an older dog, Sam, a Border terrier, like Brendan's friend

Duggie.

Sam is thirteen and is struggling a bit as he has arthritis. They seem to spur each other on and start playing the weeing game, competing to see who can wee on the most things. I know Brendan will win. He always wins. He has medals for it. Having the nice ladies to chat to also makes the walk seem easier for me. Brendan is always fine with little dogs. He only attacks bigger dogs, especially *much* bigger dogs. He's the opposite of a bully, whatever that is. An idiot probably. A few minutes later he proves this by snarling and barking like a maniac at a nice black Labrador called Jeff. Poor Jeff lollops away with his tail between his legs. He isn't too put-out; as everyone knows, Labradors are very forgiving.

At some point Brendan realises – using his built-in radar and GPS – we're now heading back towards the car. He suddenly finds a reserve of energy and runs the rest of the way.

In the car park there is a café. I get an americano and sit outside. Brendan has one of his cigars and a sausage roll. A car moves slowly past us, looking for a space. Brendan starts barking and jumping up and down frantically. He has a fear of slow-moving vehicles. Fast-moving ones are acceptable to him, but slow ones always get this reaction. I always assume he thinks they're going slowly because they're trying to kidnap him. He was captured by the dog warden in Bulgaria at some point, which presumably goes some way towards explaining his hatred of vans, any slow-moving vehicle, men in uniform, men carrying anything that resembles a stick, and usually men in general. The offending car moves on and he calms down again.

I realise he hasn't eaten any of the treats I've given him while I've been sipping my foul coffee; they're laid out in a row on the ground in front of him. It looks like he's opened a museum of dog treats and like any curator worth his salt, he isn't eating any of the exhibits.

We return to the van – along with the Dog Treat Museum – and drive around the rest of the east side of the lake. It's very nice, very pastoral, a patchwork of fields, hawthorn hedges, little whitewashed stone cottages, church spires and a lot of autumn colours. It looks like the seasons have given up their pretence and autumn is showing its true colours. Bassenthwaite looks a lot more autumnal than anywhere else we've visited so far.

I manage to park at the head of the lake and we walk along the shore. There are great views; it's such a beautiful looking lake, very green, surrounded partly by pine forests, partly by deciduous woodlands. There are several paddleboarders on the glassy water and a small group of swimmers, who are repeatedly saying things like: "Holy shit, it's f-f-f-freezing!"

While I sit and soak in the view, Brendan avails himself of the salad bar and eats enough grass to stuff a king-size mattress. He takes a break from grass-eating to stand and stare into space for a while, then resumes the grass-foraging.

As noon approaches, it's clouding over. It looks like it's going to pour down. Well, once we're on our site it can do what it likes, because Nicky has booked us on a very expensive site tonight as a treat. We'll have views over Derwentwater, attractive grounds, Wi-Fi and luxury facilities. As we'll have electric hook-up, everything that can be charged will be charged. Including Brendan. When I revealed all this to him earlier, he was so excited he had to have an immediate lie down.

On the way to the site, we call in at Castlerigg Stone Circle. The lane is packed out with cars but I manage to park some distance away. As I pull on the handbrake the heavens open and it pours down. It's a torrent of biblical proportions and there is a screaming exodus, people – already soaked – are running hysterically along the lane to their cars. Headlights light up, engines roar and cars speed away. I decide we'll give it a while for the rain to go off and I have some tomato and basil soup and sourdough bread while Brendan continues his napping. He's got it off to a fine art now; he can be in a deep hypnotic trance in under a minute.

The rain doesn't go off and it's hammering on the lane. I think we should just go for it, but Brendan looks out of the window and makes it quite clear that if I'm planning to get out, I'll be going by myself. I concede. We do a very slow drive-by and can see the stones standing on their small plain, covered in pouring rain. The land has gone dark and the sky is an eerie white. It's quite ominous. There is a slight rumbling of thunder. If I go out to the stones, I will be the tallest thing on the plain by far and whilst I'm often the tallest thing by far, that doesn't usually run the risk of a lightning strike.

We arrive at our site: our very expensive site. It's quite gorgeous. The toilets are warm and have piped music –

always a bonus. There are ornamental lawns with views over Derwentwater and well-tended borders. Our pitch is at the end of a row and we have hedges and trees on two sides. Most of the other vans and caravans seem to have people in them, looking out at the rain.

I wind the awning out and Brendan sits on the grass in a spot sheltered by the trees, but then there is a solitary clap of thunder. I didn't think it was too bad, but Brendan disagrees. He retreats to the van and lies in his basket trembling. The rain comes pelting down, hammering on the roof, which further alarms Brendan. I close the curtains and I coax him on to the settee. I play some calming dog music via YouTube, which is alright for a few minutes, but then the signal drops – perhaps because of the storm – and it stops completely, so I sing to him instead, which really appears to be helping. He seems to be calming down. Possibly because my singing proves to him there are worse things than thunder.

I love extremes of weather and I love being inside and looking out at a storm or a raging sea. I'd love to sit here now and look out at the deluge, but Brendan doesn't like it... He doesn't seem to like most things. I always put my dog first, so the curtains remain tightly closed and I completely miss the visual spectacle of the storm.

After about half an hour, the thunder has definitely passed and the rain has eased. I'm still singing and Brendan seems calmer. He's looking at me curiously; he looks perplexed actually, watching me as I'm singing to him, as though to say "In what way do you think that's helping?"

I stop singing and tease open the curtains. The awning at the side is hanging down, like a swollen bladder, filled with water. Instead of the water running off it, as it should do, it has gathered up enough to fill a large washbasin. I go outside, leaving Brendan safely inside, and try to adjust the awning so the water will drain away, but something goes wrong and one of the metal supports hits me on the head. Unlike my Honister Pass experience many years ago, I don't appear to be concussed or anything. I successfully manage to drain the awning and I set it at such an angle that there is a severe gradient on it, so it will drain. Unfortunately, this means the front is so low that every time I go towards the van I bang my head. Again. It soon stops being fun. For me anyway, I'm not sure Brendan isn't enjoying it.

The rain has definitely stopped and the sky is growing brighter, so we set off for a walk to fully explore the site. Everywhere is soaked and there is the constant running of water, draining from gutters, dripping from trees, running along the roadways. Brendan is sniffing intently at every tree and bush and lamppost. The storm means every trace of any other dog has been well and truly washed away. I thought this would be disappointing for him, but he assures me this is perfect; it's like a blank canvas and he sets about creating his masterpiece. Before long he has scent-marked and claimed the whole site as his own.

We pass the ornamental lawn. There is a view over Derwentwater, which has ribbons of mist suspended above it. It looks so beautiful and ethereal. As I'm marvelling at the view, I notice Brendan has tensed and is staring across the lawn. Something is moving across the well-trimmed grass. I assume it's a squirrel or rabbit, but it isn't. It's like a small, low racing car, suitable for a gerbil or possibly underdeveloped guinea pig. It's coming directly towards us. It's black and seems to have eyes. As it comes nearer, it's more like a tank than a racing car; a tank with headlight eyes and it looks quite demonic, like a low-slung dalek. It's still on target for us, growing ever nearer. Weirdly, Brendan is staring but isn't barking and jumping up and down. I realise it's a robotic lawn-mower.

"They're fascinating things, aren't they?"

I swing round. A staff member is passing by, smiling.

"Oh god, they really are taking over."

"Yes," he says cheerfully. "Won't be long."

He walks off, whistling, and leaves us to our collision. Still it's coming. Ten feet away. Eight feet. Five feet. Brendan is staring, incredulous. Three feet. I'm just about to drop-kick it into the lake, when – at the very last minute – it turns on a sixpence and heads off in another direction.

Still without a word from Brendan, we walk on and continue our tour of the site. We check out the guests' lounge, which is empty. It's got a gentleman's club feeling to it, with a fireplace, oak beams and dark leather chairs and sofas. And a chandelier. Brendan lies down in front of the fire. He thinks he's finally where he belongs. He'll be disappointed when he gets back to his van.

We have a lazy evening. We have several more short walks. I'm surprised to see that even after dark,

Brendan's friend Robot Mower is still at work, ploughing relentlessly up and down, now with his headlights on! This time Brendan *does* start barking, so we hurriedly leave.

I realise we made a mistake going in the guests' lounge earlier, because now it's part of Brendan's routine. Every time we venture out, we have to call in so he can stretch out in front of the fire.

* * * * * * * * * *

If Brendan Was A Human...

Human Brendan would stay in bed very late in the mornings and go to bed very early at night. He would probably lounge around in sweat-pants all day watching *Bargain Hunt*. Apart from the sweat-pants, I've just summed up Canine Brendan's ideal Saturday.

ABOVE: Mountain Brendan having a rest above Thirlmere.

ABOVE: After the storm: the view over beautiful Derwentwater.

BELOW: Derwentwater and ferry.

ABOVE: Brendan admires his reflection. And why not? It's a mighty fine reflection.

CHAPTER 8: LONELY
AS A CLOUD

In which Brendan visits the majestic Ullswater and the remote and atmospheric Haweswater. He is complemented on his "rugged good looks", so it's just an ordinary day really.

There was heavy rain in the night, hammering on the roof of the van. Because he was comfortable in his basket and sleepy, Brendan decided not to be bothered by it. And that's good news because I think we're going to get a lot of it.

We drive through spitting rain to Ullswater, the second largest lake in the Lake District, second in command, answerable only to Windermere. We park up and head for a walk along the shore. There's no wind, but it's a dull, grey, overcast day. We pass a group of ladies who have presumably just been for a cold-water swim. They stand in towelling robes, cradling hot drinks. It's all the rage now – the cold-water swimming, that is: the towelling robes are optional.

Ullswater is very verdant and attractive, with high wooded fells on the other side. Oak trees hang over the shore, dropping their leaves into the water. We wander along the lake's edge lonely as two clouds, that float on high o'er vales and hills. Yes, Ullswater has a strong Wordsworth association, as it was here that the poet saw a crowd, a host of golden daffodils. They were beside the lake, beneath the trees and – by all accounts – they were fluttering and dancing in the breeze. I'm not sure why he was making such a fuss; we have daffodils at Brendan's Field but we don't go on about it.

We are in approximately the right area, where William and his ever-present sister, Dorothy, were confronted by the discoing spring flowers. They were returning to their home in Grasmere after spending the night in Pooley Bridge, at the head of the lake, a distance of 25 miles! And Brendan complains on the way back from the field!

There are no daffodils around at this time of year – dancing or otherwise engaged – so we drive a few miles further into the village of Glenridding. There isn't a lot here in the way of facilities, there are a couple of shops, but that's about it. It's very pleasant though, made up of handsome buildings with stone walls and slate roofs, with a river running through the centre. It reminds me of a Swiss village, which perhaps isn't all that surprising as it nestles in the shadow of the mighty Helvellyn, one of the most formidable peaks in the region. I'd love to climb it.

I confess this to Brendan. "I'd love to climb that, boy." I say.

Brendan is sniffing a stone wall and conveniently can't hear me, but then he spots a lady with a female dog on a lead, miraculously all his senses return and he wants me to introduce him. I try my best, but the lady pulls her dog away.

"I'm sorry, she's a grump on the lead. She's quite tetchy. She's thirteen."

"Are you sure?" I say incredulously. "She looks like a puppy!"

"Why, how old's he?"

"Ten."

Brendan is standing proudly; he's smoothed down his fur, his eyes are sparkling, his tongue is lolling, his nose is wet, his tail is pointing skywards and he's doing his best to look nine-and-a-half.

"Well, *he* looks like a puppy." He's pulled it off! "He's got those rugged good looks. He's never going to show his age."

Brendan walks away with his head high, displaying his rugged good looks. I have to say, half the time he acts like an octogenarian, hobbling along, yawning and sitting down at every opportunity, but right now he does look like a matinee idol.

We walk through the village – I'm really looking for a café – but the village suddenly ends. That was Glenridding. I let Brendan off his lead in a park so he can have a run. Of course, he doesn't have a run; he has a sit down. We're overlooking the lake and the steamer pier. Ullswater provides an excellent ferry service. There is no better way to see this beautiful, tranquil lake than by boat. Only a fool would pass up the opportunity. I glance at Brendan, but he's made it quite clear that our options for this morning range from sitting down in this park to lying down in this park and in no way include any form of boat travel.

To thwart his plans of relaxing though, a couple walk past with a standard poodle – not that I've ever seen a sub-standard one. The dog is white and fluffy and called something unpronounceable. The dog bounds up to Brendan, disturbing his sit down and causing him to stand-up. The couple are smiling and laughing at the dogs. I'm not. Their dog is jumping backwards and forwards gleefully, trying to encourage Brendan to play. Brendan was on his break and he has strict rules about his break times. He is so affronted he's just standing there open-mouthed.

While we're talking and the dogs are now staring at each other, another woman approaches with her little dog. She ignores the poodle; she can't take her eyes off Brendan – probably admiring his rugged good looks.

"He's gorgeous. What's he called?"

"Brendan... he came with his name."

She laughs. "Oh... that's a *great* name! There are no other Brendans, are there?"

"Oh no... There are no other Brendans."

Her little dog is running around the park like a rocket, trying to get the two boys involved and succeeding, so Brendan and the poodle and the little dog are all playing together and interacting; it's so nice to watch. It's the first time Brendan has played with another dog on this trip.

"She's full of energy!" I say. "Is she young?"

"Sixteen months."

"Ah… That explains it. I ran around like that when I was sixteen months old."

"I ran around like that when I was sixteen *years* old…" the woman says suggestively, then adds a little sadly. "Wish I still could."

The couple wander away with the poodle, so we head back towards the village and the lady follows us. We start talking. She's in her sixties, not that she looks it. We get onto the subject of campervans. She has an ex-ambulance that she's partially converted herself. It turns out I've parked behind her in the village. I tell her we had intended to do a lot of wild camping in our van, but because it's been so busy and there was literally nowhere to park, we haven't managed it so far, and now my enthusiasm for it has dwindled.

"I stop in laybys all the time." she says forcefully. "I never have any trouble. Well… until the other day. I pulled up on an industrial estate to make a brew and a fat ginger woman banged on the window and said 'Hey what d'you think you're doing?' I said 'I'm having a brew and a Gypsy Cream, what're *you* doing?' She said 'You can't stop here overnight!' I said 'I'm not doing, I just told you I'm having a brew!' 'Well, you'll have to go!' 'Not until I've finished my brew, I won't!' 'You'll have to go! I'll get the owner.' I said 'Get who you like! I'm having a brew!' And I shut the curtain on her. She was just a fat ginger bitch!" Her eyes flare. "I know you shouldn't say that. But she was fat. And ginger. And a bitch."

She directs me to a café she knows, which is hidden away across a car park and seemingly in another time zone – many decades ago. It turns out to be a hotel which is open to non-residents. All the windows are covered with heavy net curtains, so I can't see inside. I push open the door and usher my dog through. Brendan is thrilled, because he loves going in places. Inside places tend to have sofas and flat screen TVs and he's never one to pass up a chance for a bit of time out.

Inside is a dining room, quite formal, quite old fashioned and completely empty. There are no customers at all. There are no staff either. There's no one. It isn't very welcoming. I take a few tentative steps forward, unsure whether to proceed, because my instinct is telling me to leave. Brendan is admiring the carpet; it's quite thick and would be very suitable to stretch out on for a siesta, though he's not sure about the garish pattern.

Suddenly there is a high-pitched shriek and a woman appears in the distance along a corridor. She's coming towards us and waving her arms hysterically. In broken English she cries: "No dog! Go outside! No dog! Only drink. No food."

"Oh, I was told..."

"No, no dog! Sit outside. Under gazebo. Go now. Hot drink only."

I'm really tempted to just leave, but then I see the menu

on the wall and the words "vegan breakfast" catch my eye, so I order one and an americano.

"Yes, yes! OK. Go now!"

So, I go and sit outside under the gazebo, which is far better anyway, because inside is very like Fawlty Towers, but less relaxing and not nearly as funny. It's not somewhere I would want to spend any time.

Brendan wanders under the table, just happy to have a bit of a rest. The woman's daughter appears and brings my coffee. She's very polite and efficient, not at all like her mother. She isn't even slightly hysterical.

While I'm eating my moderate to good breakfast, a couple come and sit under the gazebo. They get points because they both say hello. The woman is very loudly-spoken whilst the man is much more subdued – and I think a little embarrassed by his loud and unsubtle wife. I don't think she intends anyone else to hear what she's saying and I don't think she wants to hurt anyone's feelings; she probably doesn't realise how loud she's talking.

The young waitress brings their food, carrying each item separately, so she has to make several trips.

"Sorry, love…" the woman says. "I asked you for sugar. And can we have salt and pepper?"

"Yes, I'm sorry."

The woman leans forward. "You think she'd bring everything together on a tray, wouldn't you? That's ridiculous, one thing at a time."

The girl smiles awkwardly.

The husband winces. He speaks very quietly. "She can hear every word you're saying!"

"What?"

"She's standing right next to you!"

"There's no point whispering. You need to speak up."

The girl turns and walks away.

It carries on like this, with the husband constantly trying to silence his wife.

"Why are you whispering all the time? I don't know what you're saying. There's no need to whisper."

When I stand up to leave, Brendan slinks from beneath the table and stretches.

The woman turns to her husband, who tenses – wondering what she's about to say.

"I didn't realise he had a dog with him."

"Yes." the husband says quietly.

She didn't realise I had a dog? For the past half hour she's been watching me put bowls of water on the floor and hand treats down and been listening-in while I chatted to Brendan. She must have heard something along the lines of: "Do you want some more water? You do? Or you don't? OK… so do you want a sausage roll? Or a cigar? No, either or… you don't get both. No, I haven't checked the FTSE Index; you can do it yourself later."

As we leave, they both look over and earn themselves another point by saying goodbye: the man very quietly, the woman very loudly.

* * * * * * * * * *

We leave Glenridding and drive back to the lakeshore, to a sheltered cove with overhanging trees. Brendan has a paddle and a drink. There is no one around. A few days ago, the lake would have been bustling and this little bay would probably have been full of people. There is evidence of several fires. There is a Corona beer bottle on a rock, complete with cap, so it looks like an unopened bottle of premium lager. However, the liquid inside is a bit too yellow to be the lager it is supposed to be. People probably came here and had barbeques… and filled empty lager bottles with piss. And yet now it's so quiet, so peaceful, I can see that on a sunny day the views and the scenery would be absolutely amazing – and it still is. Even bad weather can't eclipse the beauty of this spectacular lake.

Ullswater is a glacial ribbon lake; the valley was scooped out by a glacier driving past and then it filled with melt water. It is often referred to as a "dog-leg", as it has two bends, but the central stretch is long and straight. It was for this reason that Donald Campbell chose Ullswater to attempt to break the water speed record in July 1955. He achieved his goal in his hydroplane Bluebird K7, reaching a speed of 202 mph. This success is less famous than his 1967 attempt on Coniston Water, when he achieved a speed of around 300 mph, but it cost him his life.

Not breaking any records at all, is a tiny motorboat buzzing backwards and forwards along the opposite shoreline, stopping for a while and then starting the buzzing again, like an irritating bluebottle. Brendan watches it with interest – I'm waiting for the barking to start – but he almost immediately loses interest and yawns, then looks away.

We sit on the shingle, listening to the water lapping against the rocks. In our everyday lives, we tend to *hear* a lot but rarely actually *listen*. It's quite relaxing to focus on something specific and really listen to it, instead of allowing that constant mind chatter. Brendan is very much in the moment, though his face looks like he often isn't enjoying the moment very much.

Today is more how I thought the whole trip would be: duller weather, cooler, no sun, quieter, plenty of places to park and the bliss of solitude. This is perfect for us; we're loving Ullswater.

In the late 'Nineties, Jimmy McGovern's partly-autobiographical TV series *The Lakes* was filmed in the area, launching the careers of many future stars, including John Simm. The scenery served as a contrasting backdrop to the gritty goings-on typical of McGovern. It was quite a hit at the time.

Brendan has been very busy, sniffing literally every inch of this little bay. I admire his thoroughness. I realise eventually, that there have probably been a hundred barbeques here which have left spilt fat all over the place. I notice he's chewing something, which I think is an acorn. Acorns are very bad for dogs as they contain tannins, which can cause severe stomach upset and even lead to organ failure in extreme cases. I try to wrestle the object out of his mouth, which takes some doing, but what I eventually get out is a slobber-covered jagged chunk of bone. I throw it in the lake. Brendan is staring into the water with his mouth open. He can't actually believe what I've just done. I turn away, when I turn back I half expect to see him attired in his Scuba-gear and wading into the lake, but he isn't, he's still standing there in a state of shock.

An elderly man in a long coat wanders on to the beach. "Oh, what a lovely dog." he says.

Strangely, Brendan doesn't react to him at all. He just remains staring into the lake, mourning the loss of his bone.

The old man chuckles. "At least he is when he's behaving, eh?"

"Well, yes... he's his own dog. He does his own thing."

"Well, that's dogs, isn't it?" He smiles and wanders off through the trees. He seems like he's looking for something. Perhaps he's trying to find his bottle of lager.

I lean back against a rock and Brendan comes and sits beside me. After the big breakfast I'm quite tired and ready to go to sleep. And Brendan is *always* ready to go to sleep.

I'm feeling very relaxed. We listen again to the

movements of the water and the stirring of the leaves above us. It's quite hypnotic. I'm loving Ullswater. I love the weather as well. It's still and grey, but it's perfect. It's ethereal and suits this beautiful lake right at this moment. I'd love to walk around it; there is now a long-distance path, the Ullswater Way, but it's 20 miles in total, so it's nineteen-and-a-half miles too far for Brendan. I would have liked to walk around all the lakes, but it would never happen with my boy. That's not to say I resent him for making the trip somewhat sedentary, because I don't. He's forcing me to sit and enjoy the moment. I have so seldom in my life ever sat down and done nothing, but now – out of necessity – we're sitting and enjoying the scenery and enjoying the present and enjoying Ullswater in the best way possible.

* * * * * * * * * *

Our site for the night is above Ullswater. It's called The Quiet Site, because it strives to provide a peaceful and calm haven, and it probably would, if it wasn't for the constant noise of a strimmer, which goes on for hours, so it isn't even slightly quiet. Ironically, the Quiet Site is one of the noisiest I've ever been on. Suddenly the strident whining stops and I see the uniformed gardener walking off. It looks like he's finished for the day. But a minute later he returns, carrying a leaf-blower and the noise continues, at a slightly different pitch.

We set off for a walk around the site. Brendan meets a lively young collie – I'll call him Shep to protect his identity. Both boys are trying to ignore each other with the most aplomb. They stand angled away from each other, not looking at each other, not speaking. At first it seems like they're equally matched, but Brendan is just toying with him. Shep is too young and inexperienced; he's thinking too hard instead of using The Force. Shep's weakening. He can't take it anymore. He leaps forward, doing a play jump at Brendan. Brendan turns away. Shep's lost. He just doesn't fully realise it yet. He's desperate; he looks around for something, for anything. He tries a new approach; he cocks his leg and wees on a clump of grass. (Sedge, if I'm not mistaken.)

Brendan saunters over; he won't hurry; he's taking his time. He lazily sniffs the grass. Correct protocol should be for Brendan to also wee on the grass and supplant the youngster's scent with his own. Instead, Brendan just turns and walks away. This isn't admitting defeat; this is saying "Your wee doesn't matter. You're no threat." In human terms, this would be the equivalent of getting someone's name intentionally wrong, purposefully forgetting to send them a Christmas card and complementing them on their interior design choices by saying something like: "I love what you've done with the place. We used to have the same curtains… before we re-modernised."

Shep is beaten. He jumps backwards and forwards a few times, then he turns and trots off along the driveway, back to his caravan. Yes, *caravan.* Not campervan. "Bloody wobble-boxes!" as my dad used to call them.

Brendan rewards himself with a sit down. I sit down as well. There's a view of the lake below. The water looks very dark now and the surrounding fells are losing their colour. The clouds are suspended above, low, heavy, ominous, not moving at all. I'm sure it will rain before long.

Before long it rains. This suits Brendan fine. We run back to the van and he's asleep in a matter of minutes. And at some point, the leaf-blowing stops.

In the evening I decide to get a pizza from the on-site pizzeria. I go up to the kiosk and am disconcerted to see the young man from reception is in the kitchen throwing pizza dough, tossing it between his hands until he gets a pizza-shape, the sort of thing you see Italians do… in Italy. It just looks wrong with him being a peroxide-blond receptionist. I assume the other staff are all multi-tasking as well. I expect Strimmer Boy is back there cutting the dough with his strimmer and possibly administering parmesan with his leaf blower. Any misgivings are misplaced, because the pizza is delicious.

The Quiet Site redeems itself and lives up to its name throughout the evening. It is incredibly quiet. We don't hear a sound all night.

* * * * * * * * * *

We wake up to a dull, grey, static morning. Nicky says it's pouring down at home; I'm sure we can expect that later. Brendan had a good night and a long sleep and is now lying on the grass, having a nap to recover. I'm a bit concerned as he's done several dog stretches, holding the position for several minutes each time, which is a classic sign of a pancreatitis flare-up. The stretching takes the pressure off apparently, so I need to keep an eye on him. This has already ruined my day; his wellbeing has a huge effect on how I'm feeling.

I go through the morning ritual of putting the bed away and packing up ready for travel. When I try to get Brendan in the van he really resists and digs his paws in the ground. I encourage him and then have to drag him onboard. He sits in his basket. I sit on the floor next to him and cuddle him.

"What's the matter, boy?"

He puts a paw on my arm and looks at me in the eye without blinking. He looks so pitiful. He breaks my heart. I'm not sure what to do, but I know he is a bit of a dramatist, and he knows how to work me like a seasoned pro. I'll have to watch him closely to see whether he needs one of his big tablets, which have to be severely limited. I shut the side door and get in the driving seat. When I look round at him, he's settling down and looks comfortable.

We set off and drive along the winding road that flanks Ullswater, only a couple of miles into Pooley Bridge, an attractive small village at the head of the lake. Brendan hops out and seems energised, frenetic actually, running around and sniffing and weeing. He seems completely fine now. I'm convinced now that the hangdog eyes and the paw were just a stunt.

We cross over the eponymous bridge and stroll around the village. It's very nice, and for such a small place has a varied selection of cafes and pubs. We feel we should take advantage, so we go in a café with a terrace overlooking the river. I can see our van in the distance; there is no finer view in the whole of Lakeland. Not that Brendan agrees; if he could look across the river and see home, he would be a lot happier.

I have a coffee and a rich fruit cake. Brendan has a sit down and yawns a lot, whilst flirting shamelessly with all the dogs at the other tables. Yes, I'm pleased to report that every single table has a dog. We're in good company. I'm also pleased to report that my personal dog is amongst the best behaved. I'm as shocked as you are! Is it his advanced obedience training kicking in? No, it's the fact that he doesn't want to waste valuable sitting down time having a set-to with a Jack Russell or a miniature schnauzer.

The coffee is nice enough, whilst not being great; the rich fruit cake is a bit too rich and too fruity, but it is definitely a cake. I feel a bit sick now though and in need of a walk.

The weather hasn't got any better, but it hasn't got any worse. There are low clouds pressing down on the land, but seemingly no wind, so we set off for a long walk to the head of the lake and along the eastern shore. This isn't the kind of long walk that the Wordsworths would do, from here back home to Grasmere, but for Brendan it's a fair trek. Ullswater looks beautiful and is adorned with moored yachts. It is the happiest combination of beauty and grandeur: Wordsworth's words, not mine. But he's not wrong.

Brendan has a paddle and seems full of energy and enthusiasm. There are lots of dogs about and he scurries around introducing himself and weeing with gusto. Everyone says hello, everyone is friendly and there is a lovely atmosphere.

We meet two ladies walking a beagle each. One of the dogs is blind, but snuffles around and seems very contented, as long as people don't rush up to him. They've had him a year and are so loving and protective towards him. His adoptive sister, who they've had for six years, looks after him and instinctively knows he needs special care. Like Brendan, they are both rescue dogs. Brendan introduces himself very gently and calmly, sensing the need for a very moderate approach. He sniffs the dog's muzzle and allows him to tentatively sniff him back, after which Brendan accepts him into his pack.

They ask about Brendan's past and comment on how handsome he is. It seems rude to enthusiastically agree – but I do. Sometimes – several times a day – I look at him and think "You are *so* handsome!" And he looks back at me as though to say "Yes, I know, we discussed it earlier."

Tiring of the adulation, Brendan wanders off and sits in the middle of a wooden jetty, guarding it, probably mistaking it for a bridge. This makes the ladies laugh.

"He's so funny!" He is. "And so lovely!" Also correct. "He's got quite a beagle look about him." I'm not sure about that. Several people have said he looks like a hound, which I thought was a generic term for a dog, but no one has accused him of being a beagle before. But there are worse things to be accused of.

I say goodbye to the ladies, Brendan turns towards the blind beagle. There is a brief exchange, something along the lines of:

"Goodbye Dennis! I'll never forget you!"

"My name's Dingo."

"Whatever."

And he scampers away, weaving amongst the trees on the shoreline.

We've enjoyed Pooley Bridge; we've enjoyed our morning and we've enjoyed all the dogs and the people.

"It would be nice to stay and relax, wouldn't it, Brendy?" It would be easy to go for another coffee, then have a pub lunch… have a stroll, sit on a jetty, have a pub tea… "But we ought to press on. Oughtn't we?" Brendan looks shocked and clearly disagrees.

But we press on regardless – a bit reluctantly – for Haweswater. I have visited once, on my own, and found it quite oppressive and lonely. Photographs of the lake and valley make me feel cold and the weather really won't be helping it today. I'm expecting it to be my least favourite lake. Also going against Haweswater, is the long and arduous journey to get there. It's another dead-end road down a dead-end valley. I'm not looking forward to it.

We set off, turning down a minor lane signed for Askham. It's very narrow and getting narrower. An old man is walking towards us. To let us pass, he climbs the grassy bank. He gives me a strange smile, a knowing smile, which I take to mean "Fool. You'll not get anywhere this way in that vehicle."

We successfully pass him and the road gets even narrower. There's now grass growing in the middle, which isn't encouraging.

"I don't like the look of this, Brendan!" I say.

He couldn't care less. He hasn't liked the look of anything since we left home.

We press on. I'm dreading another vehicle coming towards us, but none do and thankfully we reach a junction and turn onto a main road. I call it a main road, it's just a lane, quite a small lane, but a motorway compared to the last one.

We eventually come to the village of Askham, with it's wide, open, grassy centre, lined with solid but very attractive houses. I remember it distinctly, though I've only been here once and that must be two decades ago. The memory is a strange thing.

We leave Askham behind and continue along narrowing, winding lanes, rising steadily. Suddenly we're on top of the world; there are unspoilt views in all directions, pastoral views, stone walls, fields, little streams, isolated farmhouses and cottages. It's very attractive countryside, but it feels very remote, isolated. It feels very far away from civilisation. Probably because it is. It feels like we're

driving ever-further away from the 21st Century, going back in time. This bucolic view has probably remained completely unchanged for years, for whole lifetimes.

There are heavy unbroken clouds above, and then the first spattering of rain on the windscreen. We cross over several little humpbacked bridges. I'm driving very slowly to make the journey as smooth as possible for

Brendan in the back. He's awake, but lying down in his basket. The road continues to rise and then I see through the trees on my right, a glimpse of the dam and Haweswater itself.

We park in a layby, high above the reservoir. Brendan hops out with enthusiasm and leads me to a gate that's signed for the Corpse Road. Mountain Brendan is in the house! We set off up the fairly steep path, zig-zagging up the fell between bracken. Brendan scampers ahead, bouncy and full of life, but he waits for me at every turn in the path. This is a very different dog to the pitiful animal who put his paw on my arm this morning.

I'm no match for Mountain Brendan. After a few minutes it's again *me* wanting a sit down, not him; he seems to see it as an inconvenience. But we sit together and I take a good look down at the valley and the reservoir. The water level doesn't seem very high, but there's a lot of water pouring in via several inlet channels, coming down from the surrounding high fells. The bleached white limestone chippings around the upper reaches make it look undeniably like a reservoir rather than a natural lake.

There is a fringe of trees around the water, dark fir trees and the water looks black. The clouds are low and it's spitting lightly. Everything is looking very grey. The clouds are coming down and cutting off the tops of the fells, yet it doesn't look nearly as foreboding as I was expecting, as I remembered. And yet I don't actually remember much about coming here. I remember the journey very well, almost every detail of it, but I don't remember the reservoir or the valley at all.

When I stand up, I'm surprised that Brendan bounds off uphill, not downhill. He's choosing to carry on further. This hardly ever happens! I really don't know him anymore. We keep going up; he is far ahead of me, but waits, and I can see his head peering down at me from a carefully chosen vantage point. When I catch up, we have another sit down.

The view over Haweswater is getting better as we get higher. At the bottom end is the 36-metre-high dam which created the reservoir we see today; the largest reservoir in the northwest and one of the largest in England. A 56-mile-long aqueduct carries water to Manchester, terminating – like Thirlmere – in the reservoir at Heaton Park. Yes, it was the Mancs again who built the dam – completed in 1940 – which flooded the natural small lake of Haweswater and drowned two picturesque villages.

Hundreds of people were moved from their homes in Measand and Mardale Green. Unlike Thirlmere – where there was a minority of well-organised resistance – there was *huge* opposition to the Haweswater scheme. The villagers didn't want to go, but eventually the Manchester Corporation won and the valley was abandoned.

The village was demolished by the Royal Engineers, who were granted permission to use it for demolition practise. They blew it up. All except the church; 97 bodies were exhumed and reburied elsewhere. The building itself was dismantled stone-by-stone and used in the construction of the reservoir's outlet tower. It's a nice touch, an attractive building, just visible from the side of the road at certain points. It means that part of Mardale Green lives on.

In very dry summers, the ruins of the village emerge from the murky waters. There are immaculate drystone walls that have been submerged for nearly a century, still perfectly intact, along with the ruined outlines of the blown-up pub and houses. I think for this reason I find the Haweswater reservoir and valley quite sad and quite chilling.

Along with Thirlmere and a couple of reservoirs in the Peak District, Haweswater contributes to my very own tap water, so I can't complain too much or I'd go thirsty. By all accounts, Mardale was a beautiful valley and the lost villages were very picturesque. To me it feels haunted. And lonely. That doesn't mean I don't like it, because I do. I'm surprised, but I really like it. I like its atmosphere, its drama and its rather stark beauty; those qualities give it a certain melancholy splendour of its own – my words, not Wordsworth's. It has a history and a depth – other than the 60 metres of icy water that sit in the valley bottom below.

I stand up again and the same thing happens: Brendan shoots off uphill. This is really unprecedented. We climb higher and higher along the Corpse Road. Originally there was no church in Mardale, so the dead were taken for burial in Shap. A coffin was strapped to the back of a packhorse and transported via this path, over the moors.

I head off downhill, calling Brendan to follow. But he doesn't follow. He's springing off uphill, his ears and tail just visible above the curling bracken.

"Come on, boy! Brendan, come on!"

He stops and watches me as I walk further away downhill, but he still doesn't follow. He's stopped going upwards, which is good, and is now sitting down at a vantage point where he can keep an eye on me, but he's showing no sign of following me. I call him again and I beckon him. I whistle him. He's sitting tight, watching silently, but showing no signs of being about to give in.

We're both stubborn. I can't back down now. I keep walking casually away, further downhill. I go round a corner and he's lost from sight. I stop walking and wait. I can't go back, but I feel very uncomfortable not being able to see him. I'm just about to set off back upwards, when his head appears over a rock above me, checking where I am. This is a partial victory; he's shown weakness.

It's time to play my ace; use the ultimate weapon again. I haven't used it for a while now, so it's due an airing. I take off my rucksack and sit down. In less than a minute he's sitting beside me. He can't resist a group sit down. He couldn't get here fast enough. Other dogs can be bribed by edible treats or a ball or other toy, but mine responds to sit-downs.

I ask him if he wants a sausage roll; he does and he wolfs it down. This is odd because he really isn't usually bothered about them. This is new Mountain Brendan. Unfortunately, that was the very last treat. We've run out.

We have a short sit down and then – it's as though I haven't learned anything. I set off downhill, but he doesn't follow. I stop at a suitable place and crouch down. I don't take my rucksack off and I'm clearly not comfortably seated and relaxed. He can tell the difference between a real sit down and a fake sit down. And he isn't coming. I give up and sit down properly. He comes hurtling towards me. We have a sit down and I put his lead on.

He will not willingly walk back downhill towards the van. I think the whole Mountain Brendan thing is him trying to keep out of the van as long as possible. He really doesn't like it.

We reach the lane and he is really starting to drag. Regardless of how slowly he's going, we eventually and inevitably arrive back at our nameless van. I open the side door and he jumps in, but keeps hopping out whenever he sees an opportunity. He really hates this van.

We have lunch with a view over the dark and brooding lake. Down the lane I can see quite an elderly chap setting off up the Corpse Road. He's alone and it seems quite foolhardy to be doing that walk alone in weather that's very unpredictable. He disappears from view.

When Brendan is fully recharged, he sits up and looks at me, so we set off for a walk in the other direction, along the road – again it was Brendan's choice – and we're walking uphill *again*. Very dark clouds are gathering above.

We find a rocky outcrop amongst flowering heather, with a view over the lake, which proves to be the perfect place for a sit down. Along the shoreline I can just see the water tower that incorporates the stone from the church; it's an elegant, castellated structure.

Beside me, Brendan suddenly starts barking and staring at the lane. I glance over and see the old chap who had set off on the Corpse Road. He waves and calls over to us and starts chatting. He's staying at the Haweswater Hotel, which was built in 1937, during the dam construction, to replace the lost pub in Mardale Green. It's positioned half way along the lake and classes itself as an art deco hotel, featuring roofing slates and other embellishments rescued from the village.

The old chap tells us he had started up the Corpse Road, but had slipped a few times and thought he was going to end up seriously injuring himself. "And if I do, I won't be found for hours."

If ever. And the Corpse Road… There's an ominous clue in the title.

"I used to walk here all the time… all these fells…" He looks around wistfully. "But I haven't been walking for four years now… Anno Domini is beating me somewhat." He sounds quite dispirited. "Ah well… How about you? Where have you walked to today? I bet you're up and down these fells every day, aren't you?"

I have never felt so flattered, whilst also feeling disappointed in myself.

"Not really. We've hardly been anywhere."

We chat for a while longer and then he sets off jauntily back to his hotel.

The spot we're sitting is actually a well-known filming location, to which many pilgrims come to visit re-enact a much-loved scene. The film is the 1987 black comedy *Withnail and I*, starring Richard E. Grant and Paul McGann. It was filmed in and around the area. The scene features out of work actors, Withnail (Grant) and flatmate Marwood (McGann), standing above the lake in the gathering dusk, and Withnail theatrically booming across the valley "I'm going to be a star!" Whilst Richard E. Grant would certainly become a star, it is unlikely that Withnail would ever make it. The film was a box office flop, but went on to become a cult classic. I've tried several times, but never managed to get through it.

It's getting darker by the second. The black clouds are spreading out over the valley. I'm pretty sure it's going to leather it down before long.

Looking down, I can clearly see how the water goes very deep, very quickly. It turns from sandy-coloured to dark and impenetrable. It's weird to think that once there were two villages down there, and that their remains still exist, submerged in the darkness. I think that's one of the things that has always unsettled me about Haweswater: that it's a reservoir and it covers two former villages, so it seems like a haunted place. It destroyed a way of life and disenfranchised people, but the ghostly remains are still there, unseen but real nevertheless.

Also, its remoteness is quite daunting and thrilling. I think it's more remote and isolated than Wastwater, which at least has a few houses and farms, a pub and a campsite. At the head of the valley, Haweswater has nothing. It's not on the way to anywhere and it feels like it's really out on a limb.

On our way back to the van, we meet three elderly ladies who have walked here from Ullswater, near where we started from. They have walked right over the high fells. They try to show me the route, but most of it is now lost in dark clouds.

"It was retched on the tops…"

"Oh, it was evil!"

"Just awful!"

I'm so impressed with them doing the walk at all, it must have been terrible in weather like this.

Two of them try to stroke Brendan and he barks at them to warn them off. I feel so embarrassed because, as usual, they were trying to be nice, but they did it for too long.

They set off along the lane towards the hotel, where they're being picked up. I tell them to look out for the old chap and say hello to him.

Rain is blowing in the wind as we head back to the van. Brendan's had a very busy day and he's tired. This time he has no problem slinking into his basket and staying there.

Tonight's site is large and functional. It's getting colder. We have a relaxing night in. Apart from a few sniff walks around the site, Brendan keeps his head low.

* * * * * * * * * *

If Brendan Was A Human...

Human Brendan – like Canine Brendan – would always side with the underdog.

ABOVE: Brendan having a sit down, with the head of Haweswater in the background.

ABOVE: Brendan, never knowingly not sporting a hang-dog expression.

ABOVE: Storm clouds gather.
(I'm talking about the weather rather than Brendan's mood.)

ABOVE:The head of Haweswater: the drowned valley.

ABOVE: Beautiful Ullswater.

ABOVE: Ullswater, close to where Wordsworth wandered lonely as a cloud and famously spotted the daffodils.

ABOVE: Ullswater: Brendan tries to remember where he parked his yacht.

CHAPTER 9: WORDSWORTH'S LAKES

In which Brendan follows in the footsteps of the Lake poets * and lo! visits Grasmere and Rydal Water: "the loveliest spot that man hath ever found".

* (Not literally – they tended to walk much too far for Brendan!)

Disclaimer: No sonnets were harmed during this visit. Well, hardly any.

It's around 2am. It's so cold. I lie awake freezing for a couple of hours, trying to pull the duvet around me tighter and block out any cold air seepage, but I've had to give in and put the heater on and add extra layers, including a hooded top. That's better but my head's still freezing so I've had to put the hood up. I can't believe the sudden change in temperature. Brendan is curled up really tightly in his basket. I wish he could come up on the bed; he wishes he could come up on the bed. We are unanimous.

Because it was cold last night, I had put the reflective windscreen insulation on. Like the awning, I've never had one before. It's supposed to keep the cold out and keep the heat in. Unfortunately, the front windows were still open, but it's difficult to tell with the insulation on. This explains why it was freezing in the night. I try to close the windows without Brendan noticing; I don't want to give him something to moan about all day. (Something *else* to moan about; he's got quite a list.)

We set off heading to Grasmere via Keswick. We're taking a longer route in the hope that it will be easier and less undulating for Brendan. The sun has come out, it's warmed up and it looks like it's going to be a beautiful day.

At one point a female cyclist – dressed from head to toe in pink dayglo gear and matching helmet – suddenly cuts onto the carriageway directly in front of us,without looking. We swerve to avoid her, which disrupts Brendan's nap. She realises her mistake – disturbing Brendan whilst napping – and veers off at a sharp tangent. Apart from this, the journey is uneventful.

I decide, as we're passing close to Castlerigg stone circle, we'll stop and have a proper look at it. It's before 9.30, so while I don't expect it to be deserted, I do expect it to be fairly quiet. However, there is a stream of cars parked along the lane and there is even an ice cream van! An ice cream van! At 9.30 in the morning!

When I first came to Castlerigg, I was in my teens; it was a fairly secret place then, only frequented by hippies and weirdos. And sometimes weird hippies. You would usually find yourself alone or with just one or two other people. It now seems to have really taken off and be right on the tourist map. Most people don't seem to stay long; they take a photo, walk around – evidently have an ice cream for breakfast – and then leave. It is now the most-visited stone circle in Cumbria.

Brendan gazes around at the field and the stones. I know that look: "Oh wow! Somewhere else I'm not even remotely interested in!" He sits down heavily.

It's a mysterious and mystical place which needs to be experienced in near-solitude to fully appreciate it. It's a dramatic location: a little plain surrounded by high fells, creating a natural amphitheatre. The stones are arranged in a flattened circle with a 30-metre diameter, so it's quite a sizeable monument. It was constructed around 3200 BCE in the Late Neolithic period.

I try to walk around the circumference with Brendan, but he goes into a mood because I won't let him wee on the megaliths. He throws himself down in the grass again and refuses to move. I use the opportunity to try and count the stones, as tradition states it is impossible and you will arrive at a different number each time. There are around 40. But there may only be 38. But there might be 42. It does seem to be impossible, so let's stick with "around 40".

A group of Chinese tourists are taking photos of each other amongst the stones. They suddenly leave and for a moment I'm completely alone, for a matter of seconds and then the Deathwish Cyclist arrives in her pink superhero outfit. She takes a quick selfie and then cycles off.

A lovely Geordie couple arrive and stop to admire Brendan. They have a little Patterdale terrier with them – I only know he's a Patterdale because they tell me. He's called Finn and, like Brendan, he's a rescue dog. He's 11 with a lovely white muzzle and wise eyes. They've had him for 10 years now, so most of his life. He has a few health problems including epilepsy. They absolutely love him and it's so nice talking to them. Brendan wags his tail while greeting Finn for a minute and then walks off, turns his back on everyone and sits down. It seems the Neolithic period is not one that holds a special interest for him.

* * * * * * * * * *

We arrive in Grasmere in the mid-morning, before it's completely packed out. As we're walking towards the village centre, two older gents overtake us. I'm about to say hello, but they say it first.

"Hello. Beautiful day!"

"Cracking weather!"

"It is!" I call gleefully after them as they retreat. It's made my day.

We enter the first café we come across. Brendan gratefully stretches out under the table. I have Italian lemon cake – presumably from Italy – and an americano. Not from America – from Puerto Rico. The young waiter is very polite and trying hard, but he keeps getting people's orders wrong.

"I'm sorry, did you say white toast?"

"Brown."

"Oh, brown. Sorry"

Continually wrong.

"Excuse me, did you say tea or coffee?"

"I said hot chocolate."

"That's right. I'm sorry."

"Flat white?"

"No… Black coffee."

"That's right. Sorry. Is that with hot milk or cold, or cream, or lemon?"

"*Black* coffee! Without milk or cream or lemon!"

I think his nerves are ruining it for him, but he's trying hard.

The lemon cake doesn't taste of Italy – it doesn't conjure memories of summers spent in Tuscany – it doesn't even taste of lemons, which should be a given. It tastes of sage and onion stuffing, which is very odd. And the americano doesn't taste of America, or Puerto Rico – or even coffee. It's very, *very* bad.

We leave, feeling a bit sick. We try to walk to the lake, so Brendan can have a paddle and an inevitable sit down, but you have to walk half a mile along a road with no pavement and the road is too busy, so we have to abort. We'll have to try again tomorrow via a different route. Instead, we return to Grasmere and wander around the village in the sunshine. Over the years, I've visited and stayed at Grasmere more than anywhere else in the Lakes.

It was probably the first lake and village I got to know well.

Grasmere is synonymous with Wordsworth, though he only actually lived here for 14 years in total. He referred to it as "the loveliest spot that man hath ever found". Certainly, enough people seem to agree with that, as it's getting busier by the second.

While no stranger to the odd limerick, Brendan isn't up to speed on British poets, so I try to fill in a few of the blanks. Wordsworth – known to his friends as William – was born in Cockermouth, which was then in Cumberland, in 1770. He was educated at Hawkshead Grammar School and then Cambridge, after which – like Brendan – he travelled fairly extensively. In revolutionary France he did a bit more than travel and fashioned himself a daughter. He met Samuel Taylor Coleridge in the West Country and they formed a lifelong friendship. I'm talking about Wordsworth, you understand, not Brendan; as far as I know, Brendan has never met Coleridge.

Wordsworth returned to his roots in what is now Cumbria, living at various places around the central Lakes. For the last seven years of his life he was Poet Laureate. He died in 1850. He remains one of the most celebrated English poets and nearly everyone can manage a quote from "the Daffodils". Brendan *loves* daffodils. In all seriousness, daffodils are his favourite flower – to wee on. When he sees any he goes into a weeing frenzy. But you probably don't need to know that.

I've been to Grasmere many times, the first that I can remember being on the school holiday when we stayed in four different youth hostels. It rained a lot and most of the time I recall thinking "Why did I consent to this?" A year later I repeated the trip with friends. As I recall, it rained a lot then as well. We stayed in the same youth hostels and existed almost entirely on tinned sponge puddings. Every day, sponge puddings. Never got sick of them. Why would you?

I used to stay in Grasmere with Nicky on a regular basis, self-catering usually, sometimes in B&Bs. Most of the shops and cafes have changed since then. It's very different. It's almost like a different village.

Grasmere is relatively quiet, but still too busy for Brendan. A man – a tourist – dressed completely in purple, bumps into us in the street – we literally collide. When he sees Brendan, he theatrically throws his arms in the air and stands mouth-agape.

"Oh... my... *god*! He's *gorgeous*! What kind of dog is he?"

"He's a rescue, a street dog, so he could be anything... or everything."

He bends down and grabs Brendan by the head, rigorously rubbing the sides of his face. Time freezes. I've seen this so many times before. I'm trying to pull Brendan away before he can gather his composure and react, because he's bound to react very badly to this well-meaning assault. Thankfully, he's so shocked that he just stands there. The man stands up and has escaped a beating.

"Dogs his size – medium dogs – they just *love* me. Love me!

Love me! They can't get enough of me!" He reaches down and vigorously ruffles the thick fur on Brendan's lower back. *"I'm loving having my butt rubbed, Dad!"* he says in a squeaky voice.

We both look at him wide-eyed. I realise it's supposed to be an impression of Brendan. A bad impression. Brendan sounds nothing like that! Then he's roughly stroking his neck. This time Brendan's ready for him; he whips his head round, but I grab his muzzle and pull him out of strike range. I make hurried excuses and we walk away very rapidly.

It's made me really stressed and the ordeal has left Brendan completely speechless. We wander along the high street in something of a daze. Minutes pass, and it feels like normal life has almost been resumed, when I hear the familiar screeching:

"Oh my god! There he is! That's him!"

I turn around. Brendan turns around. Mr Purple is upon him, this time with a woman – his wife? A female friend? Possibly even a convenient stranger. We don't know. They make an unlikely pairing.

"Isn't he adorable! I wish I knew what breed he was!"

The man roughly strokes him again, and then the woman also joins in.

"He's gorgeous. Aren't you? Yes, you are!"

Brendan has reached saturation level. He really barks at them. They both fly backwards, hands on chests, mouths open.

"Oh my god…" Mr Purple exclaims with a gasp. He stares at his female companion. "He *hates* you! He absolutely *hates* you!"

"My bad." the woman says. "I should have been more careful."

"Yes!" Mr Purple agrees. "You should!"

"I'm so sorry," I say, "but he's really nervous."

"We should have known better. That was irresponsible of us. I'm sorry little fella…" She reaches out a hand to console Brendan, then thinks better of it and withdraws it sharply.

I go into detail about Brendan's past, his fear of…. Well, virtually everything… and they're really understanding. And they don't attempt to stroke him again.

We say goodbye and continue through the village. Brendan is very much the anglophile and is desperate to see Dove Cottage, where Wordsworth lived with his sister – I'm not judging – and later also his wife. I think I went in on the school trip and years later also with Nicky. It's one of those places that you really should see while you're here. Obviously, we don't go in. I think we've had enough people-in-close-proximity action for one day.

Dove Cottage was built in the 17th century as an inn, the Dove and Olive Branch. It's an attractive little cottage built of local stone, with bright limewashed walls. It has four bedrooms, but they're very tiny. William lived here for over eight years, from 1799 to 1808. They were productive years for him, during which time he wrote much of his most famous poetry, including *I Wandered Lonely As A Cloud*. AKA *The Daffodils*. Wordsworth recalled that period as years of "plain living, but high thinking". Brendan views his last trip to his beloved field in the same way. William got married; they had three children in close succession and Dove Cottage became too small, so they moved across the village to a larger property.

Seeing as Brendan won't let us go in Dove Cottage, we return to the village centre, but it's hard going. We're missing a gradient today; we've only walked on the flat. Every other day we've done hills and it seems to really have boosted Brendan's fitness levels. Also, my back has been better than it ever is at home. My boy is currently plodding along wearily and I think an uphill stretch would really revitalise him. He keeps looking at green areas where he could have a lie down. He keeps stopping and progress is painfully slow. He also won't drink any water and it's getting very hot.

Out of desperation, we end up having a sit down in a car park, simply because we're passing and it's there, and there is a bench and a patch of lush grass. Grasmere is a beautiful historic village surrounded by breathtaking fells and the sun is shining, but we're sitting in a car park with a steady stream of vehicles pulling in and out and coach engines idling, filling the air with diesel fumes, because this is where Brendan wants to sit.

When we finally make a move, we visit the Wordsworth

graves in the shady corner of the churchyard, because Brendan wants to visit another great writer. The grave of Wordsworth himself, his wife and their children and his sister Dorothy are amongst the most-visited graves in the country. People file past and take a photograph, then move on to buy some famous Grasmere gingerbread, as purchased by diminutive actor Tom Cruise. Apparently. It seems rude not to follow in Tom's footsteps and observe this tradition, but the queue is right down the street, so I conclude it's a mission impossible and instead we compromise and go for a pub lunch.

We choose a large pub in the centre, which in my day I'm pretty sure was called the Red Lion, but now isn't. It's dim inside with lovely old wooden furniture. True to form, Brendan dives under the table and hits the cool slate floor. The soundtrack is a Britpop compilation: all the hits you know and… know. I have a plant burger, chips and salad and an alcohol-free lager. It's very nice. Even nicer than the food is the whole experience of eating and drinking in a centuries-old pub, whilst my dog snores beneath an antique table.

Outside in the sunshine, we pass Pierce Brosnan, possibly about 20 years ago, walking two lovely dogs. One male, one female. Brendan rushes up to them to say hello, then does his patented sit-down-and-snub combo.

"They look like great pals." I say. "Do they get on well?"

Pierce nods, but in a way that means 'No, not really.' "Fine, yes." he says. "Mainly fine. But no, not really. They tolerate each other mainly. She's nine, he's only one."

"So as long as he does what he's told?"

Pierce gives a broad grin. "Yep… you know the score. Same for all of us." He's still chuckling as he walks away.

I've just realised, Brendan has been on his lead all day: our early morning walk around the campsite, then Castlerigg, and around Grasmere. He's done a lot of sniffs and met a lot of dogs, but I want him to live up to his name and be a free dog and have some freedom, so we go to the park and I let him off to have a stretch and burn off some steam. He ambles into the middle of the playing field, yawns and sits down. And that's it. He doesn't move again.

I sit next to him, enjoying the sunshine and the peace. Above the treeline I can see a rocky outcrop, Helm Crag, known locally – and by most of the country who aren't remotely local actually – as the Lion and the lamb, because the rocks form the outline of a little lamb between the paws of a huge lion.

"Thank you for not eating me." the lamb is saying.

"It's OK." the lion booms back. "I'm full. I'm saving you for supper."

After Grasmere we drive to our site for the next two nights. There's a short but tightly winding way over the tops, or a much longer but slightly less winding way via the main roads. With Brendan in mind, we take the latter. I've been to this site before. I've just realised that was about ten years ago, so that would have been my last visit to the lakes. It's quite expensive, but it's a really good location and is surrounded by woodlands and good walks.

In the late afternoon, we set off on a ramble along a footpath close to the site. A couple overtake us, but Brendan is so absorbed sniffing a thistle that he doesn't even notice them.

The woman smiles. "He hasn't even noticed us!" (I told you.)

"He's very busy at the moment." I say. "Sniffing and weeing, weeing and sniffing. It never ends."

The man laughs. "Good lad!"

Brendan still hasn't reacted to their proximity. They continue along the path and are gone. He finally finishes sniffing the thistle and promptly wees on it. Job done.

Brendan requests a sit down and it's just starting to rain, so we sit under the shelter of some trees and listen to the raindrops on the roof of yellowing leaves above us. It gives me time to reflect. I'm rapidly coming to the conclusion that we'll have to get rid of the van. It's just not for Brendan. He hates this van. He hates the size and he hates the layout. He coped well with our previous van – at least in time they resolved their differences. This hasn't happened yet and I really don't think it will.

The van is too expensive to keep for the odd day trip. It's going to depreciate in value and I can't justify having a vehicle and not using it for what it's intended for. So, the logical answer is to get rid of it. That isn't the conclusion I wanted to arrive at, and yet that's where I've arrived and pulled on my metaphorical handbrake. If it's not suited to Brendan then it has to go. I run my hand through Brendan's thick fur and kiss the top of his head. He glances around warily to make sure no one has witnessed this embarrassing display of affection.

We walk a long way back through the site. There are static homes in certain areas. They are spacious and very swish with decking, balconies, French windows, expansive living rooms and massive tellies. The only thing is, the huge picture windows look out onto the driveways, so people like us can walk past and spoil your privacy. It would be quite disconcerting to glance up from your 84-inch plasma screen and see Brendan peering in, mentally critiquing your interior design choices.

It looks like the rain has set in for the evening. Brendan has his tea under the awning and then voluntarily jumps into the van and leaps gratefully into his basket. I haven't heard from him since. He seems to love his basket in the van. When it was in the house, he wouldn't go near it; it was never used. Ever.

Well, it's 9.35pm and still raining. We start our evening routine. For me that means washing up and putting everything away in its rightful place, so we have room for all the things we need at night. Then pulling the bed out. Closing all the curtains – which takes far longer than you'd think it should. Over to the shower block in the rain. Shower. Get scalded by overly hot and uncontrollable water. Get dried. Walk back in the rain; get wet again.

Brendan's routine: do nothing.

I try to relax, but at 9.15, Brendan starts barking from his basket. A caravan is being reversed into the free space beside us. There are plenty more-accessible free spaces, but they've chosen this one. And they aren't being quiet about it. It takes some time and several manoeuvres in the dark, with the wife standing shouting directions, until the caravan is in place. Brendan barks all the time. I put music on, but he still barks. He isn't used to having anyone in that space and he can't cope with changes.

I take him out for another short walk and he sniffs and wees in the darkness. When we get back the couple are banging about getting things sorted, and making no attempt to be quiet. Having checked them out, Brendan is now satisfied that they aren't assassins – they're certainly not *stealthy* assassins – and they're not part of a rival gang, here to wee on his bushes and scratch his lawn, so he gets back into his basket without another word.

We've had a long day and we're both tired. But it's been a good day on the whole, a memorable day. We drift off to sleep with the rhythmic sound of rain pattering on the roof. *

* This is just a poetic turn of phrase. As an insomniac, I lie awake for hours with the sound of rain pattering on the roof.

* * * * * * * * * *

It rained so heavily in the night. I can't believe Brendan didn't react. It was like African tribal rhythms being drummed on the roof. I tried to record it but it didn't really pick up how tuneful it was. Then this morning it's absolutely beautiful, the sun is shining and Brendan is still asleep.

We set off at nine o'clock for our first walk. Brendan's morning walk is easily his favourite. Usually. It's the only one he ever shows any enthusiasm for. Today he isn't really up for it for some reason. He saunters along half-heartedly, yawning and occasionally stopping to stare into space. He looks like a smoker who hasn't yet had his first cigarette of the day.

Despite the sunshine, it's quite cold and the air is crisp. It looks very autumnal. The hedgerows are bracken, bramble, nettles, a variety of ferns, mosses, hawthorn. I'm again astounded by the beauty of these roadside hedges, the grassy banks and undergrowth. Most of the flowers have gone now, there are just a few tired remnants of campion and herb Robert, but the brambles and hawthorns are heavy with berries.

As stunning as the hedgerows are, they fail to enthuse Brendan, so we head back to the van and set off to visit our final two lakes. We park at White Moss Common, a woodland area between Rydal Water and Grasmere. It has strong – and somewhat negative – Wordsworth connections. Always a keen walker, at the age of 80, William came here for a stroll, but ended up catching pleurisy, from which he subsequently died.

It's a lot busier than I was expecting and we have difficulty parking. It's like a weekend again; there are people everywhere, cars everywhere, dogs everywhere. We eventually find a space and set off through the trees. Brendan is now fully awake and races ahead along the meandering tree-lined path. He's thrilled to find a bridge over the river – the Rothay – which connects Grasmere and Rydal Water and then continues to Windermere. He sits down in the middle of the bridge, as usual. A terrified young couple are attempting to squeeze past him. He looks at me for guidance or reassurance – or possibly complicity. I raise a finger, pointing at him sternly. He lets them go, but is clearly enjoying their terror. I smile and say hello to them. They don't respond at all; they just walk hurriedly away.

We break the cover of the trees, and come to Rydal Water, an attractive green lake, shimmering in the sunlight. At less than a mile long, Rydal is the second smallest lake, after Elter Water – and like Elter Water it is very accessible and has a very popular public footpath alongside. It can get horrendously busy here.

There is a really nice walk around it, taking in two of Wordsworth's homes and a variety of scenery, but glancing at Brendan, I already know we won't even be attempting it. *

* I'm developing a new book genre: non-travel writing. We'll tell you all the places we *haven't* visited and go into detail about what we didn't do when we weren't there. I wanted to walk around the lake via the lovely path on the other side, but Brendan isn't up for it, so we don't do it.

In the middle of the lake is an exposed rock, with a cormorant standing on it, but not with his wings out-stretched in the classic pose. There are two swans standing on either side staring intently at him, trying to intimidate him, but he's holding his ground. Brendan won't tolerate bullying and barks in solidarity. Neither the swans nor the cormorant react at all; they don't even flinch. They're far out enough to know they're safe from all predators – except each other. Brendan barks repeatedly – then realises the futility, so promptly stops. You can take solidarity too far.

We sit with a view over the lake. It's beautiful here. There is a brief and unexpected shower, then the rain stops, the sun comes out and it gets very hot. We continue along a well-trodden pathway, rising above the common. We end up walking behind two Geordie women, who are apparently care workers talking about their clients. Suddenly, the calm is shattered as three jet-fighters scream low overhead. Everyone automatically stares upwards and follows the planes as they recede rapidly. Brendan also looks up, but isn't too alarmed. He's getting used to them. They disappear from view and the rumbling fades.

An old man approaching, smiles and says to the two Geordies "We could do without those going over all the time, couldn't we?"

One of the women says quite aggressively. "Well, let's hope we never need 'em!"

The old man flounders; he smiles awkwardly, hesitates, seems to be frozen for a moment, then he just walks away. He appeared at first as a spritely septuagenarian enjoying the countryside, but he walks away a broken man. He will probably be dead within a week.

A few minutes later, two old prop planes fly low over the valley, following (very slowly) in the wake of the jets. It's like the same scene repeated, but from a century ago. Again, everyone looks skywards as they fly lethargically over the valley.

We pass an older couple sitting on a bench. I overhear them reminiscing. "And d'you remember we went up there on that school trip?" Could they have been together since school? Evidently so. Their conversation is tinged with sadness, as though they believe they might not come here again. I always think that of places. So, will I come here again? Will I come here again with my dog? I certainly hope so – not that he'd thank me for it.

We continue along a popular path called Loughrigg Terrace, which traverses the lower slopes of Loughrigg Fell, offering views down over Grasmere lake and village. Again, I've walked this path so many times, with various dogs and countless people. The first time was on the school trip, the second was soon after with friends. We walked from nearby High Close Youth Hostel into the nearest town of Ambleside for the sole purpose of buying those aforementioned tinned sponge puddings for our tea. Then we walked back via the terrace. That was the extent of our day's activity.

Grasmere is probably *the* most popular lake. It's the absolute epitome of Lakeland; you can't look at a calendar without seeing Grasmere. It is probably the lake I have visited most and know the best. I have many fond memories of it. I've walked along these shores countless times with Nicky and our dogs, first Cindy, then Jake. And now I'm here with Brendan. I've been boating on Grasmere with Nicky and with my childhood friends. I came to Grasmere many times with Mum and Dad. We came and stayed over Christmas one year with Nicky's mum. It snowed; it looked magical and was like being in a Christmas card. It's perhaps fitting then that it's the final lake of the trip. It wasn't intentional, it just happened that way.

From here we have a perfect view over the whole of the lake, and it really *is* perfect; the shore is surrounded by trees, which stop as the land rises, leaving very pleasing rock and bracken. The fells take the breath away. This really is a most sublime view; we have the perfect vista with so little effort. It's a beautiful lake in a beautiful setting.

This would be a gorgeous place to live. King of Pain, Sting, is reputed to have a house on the outskirts of the village, possibly next to some fields of gold. The information is so sketchy though, that I suspect it isn't true.

I'd like to walk around Grasmere, but that isn't going to happen with Brendan. He's done very well, but he's tired now. It's quite restricting travelling with an older dog, but I wouldn't change it for the world.

I wish he was a few years younger, but then again I wish I was a few years younger. However, in Brendan's case it wouldn't make him very much more active – he's always been lazy. Besides, he's done very well on this trip. Moderately well. And sitting here with my boy is good enough: my arm around him and this view over Grasmere and White Moss Common – it's close to perfection.

A nice couple appear, walking uphill towards us. The man suddenly laughs uproariously and points at us. "Look at that! Matching faces! Look! Same beard! Brilliant!"

It's possible we both look a bit woolly and unkempt at the

moment – that's the price you pay when you're an epic explorer and adventurer – but I've never really thought we were doppelgangers. Brendan seems to be offended and flies at their dog, a young, thick-set boxer. It's a male and he's big and strong, so Brendan has to show him who's boss. And he does! I have to drag him off and put him on his lead.

The couple and their dog move on – probably to start therapy sessions. We carry on with our sitting down, but then Brendan is suddenly sick: bright yellow bile. I'm sure no one's ever looked at this colour and said "George, that's the colour I want for the cushions in the conservatory." It's gaudy and – as my mum would say – lurid. Not that bile is generally known for its aesthetic quality. After the vomiting stops, he seems alright, but this has crushed my fragile mood. I feel very sad and down.

We set off back towards the van. Brendan knows we're heading vanwards, so he pulls to go in every other direction. When this doesn't work, he employs all his delaying tactics: stopping to sniff things, staring into the distance and just plain, simple sitting down. When none of these work, he just drags sulkily. We always dance to Brendan's tune and Brendan's tune is a slow waltz. Emphasis on the slow.

We spend a lazy few hours relaxing on the site. Brendan is really tired after what turned out to be a long walk. He has a nap in his basket and then a nap outside; the location is secondary to the napping, you understand.

In the early evening, we go for a walk along the footpath next to the site. The air is still, dull and grey; the light is fading long before the sun is due to set. We sit on a rock in the craggy field. I feel a sudden sense of achievement. We've completed our mission. We've visited all sixteen lakes. I've never done that before. Now it's our last evening and tomorrow we head home. Over the treetops, stretched out in the fading light I can see Windermere, where our adventure began – or our series of *mis*adventures. Brendan sits beside me, looking a bit gloomy, possibly picking up on my mood.

When our last trip – around the coast of England – was coming to an end, I did anything to postpone it. We stayed extra nights in places just to make the adventure last longer, even staying overnight when we were only a two-hour journey away from home, just to wring out the last moments of our trip together. It had been an epic adventure.

This time I don't have that feeling. This isn't a criticism of the Lakes, which are as beautiful as ever. I feel down because Brendan hasn't enjoyed the trip. He hates the van. He hates travelling and he'd rather be at home. And he's got his pancreatitis complications, he's got his special diet and his medication. He's a home-boy, he's lazy, he's getting older. He thrives on routine and daytime TV.

The atmosphere is very heavy. The light is fading steadily and the last night of our trip seems to be ending on a very reflective and sombre note. Just to complete the mood, it starts to rain. I remain seated, thinking it will go off. It doesn't go off; it gets heavier. Brendan looks at me in amazement – as though I've learned nothing. He stands up and sets off back towards the site. We run the last section, as it starts to absolutely throw it down.

It rains all night. It rains *heavily* all night. It's the kind of rain that causes floods. It never lets up. Again, there is the strange, rhythmic percussion on the roof, which reminds me of Dad. It's actually deafening and I don't sleep from about 2am, but I'm warm and comfortable.

Tomorrow gradually turns into today. It's morning. There is stark daylight. After a short walk we get back in the van, Brendan curls up in his basket and I start the engine.

* * * * * * * * * *

If Brendan Was A Human...

Human Brendan is resolute. Once he's made a decision about something it's set in stone and he is quite inflexible. This is usually because he has spent so long ruminating on the subject and working out every variable, subsequently testing it in his mental laboratory – using Litmus paper – so he is convinced he's right. It was in this way that Canine Brendan scientifically decided he didn't like travelling and nothing will shake that conviction.

ABOVE: Brendan at Castlerigg stone circle - trying to pretend he's one of the stones so he can have a nap unhindered.

ABOVE: Stunning Castlerigg. And a lazy dog.

ABOVE: Grasmere: the epitome of Lakeland.

ABOVE: Brendan having a well-deserved rest, above Rydal Water.
(For once, it really *is* well-deserved!)

CHAPTER 10: NOT DONE YET!

In which Brendan revisits Buttermere and Crummock Water – in the hope that this time he'll actually be able to park, get out of the van, have a paddle, a piddle, a sit down and a nap. Not necessarily in that order.

We drive along. Brendan is relaxed in his basket. I'm happy and excited. But not because we're going home – because we *aren't* going home. Home is to the south. We're heading north – *away* from home. We're heading back to Buttermere.

Without even discussing it with Brendan, I made an executive decision. The fact that we were unable to stop at Buttermere last time *really* annoyed me. I like a sense of completeness and this really rankled, so I decided we'd try again.

Because Buttermere is still likely to be busy and have no parking at all – and because I want to treat Brendan to some quality time in luxury at the end of our adventure – I've booked us into a hotel. I thought it would be an experience and Brendan's never stayed in one before; in the past he's never been well-behaved enough, but I think he could do it now. I *hope* he can do it now. He can't do it now, can he! No, he'll be fine. He will. Anyway, we'll find out soon enough because it's booked and paid for.

There are two hotels in Buttermere and one of them is very dog-friendly, so that's where we're going. I'm really excited about returning to Buttermere. As usual, Brendan is less excited and would rather head home and go to his field, but I've noticed how much he benefits from being away, having his routine challenged and having a lot of new sights and sounds and smells.

The last part of the journey takes us through the Newlands valley, which is quite beautiful. It was here that I came for my very first trip to the Lake District with my parents. We stayed in a large hotel, as I recall. I can't find any mention of that hotel now, so I assume it closed down years ago. On that holiday we saw mist and rain and greyness, but no sunshine. Today couldn't be more different. It's currently a beautiful sunny day and it's supposed to be nice for about a week, then it's supposed to be less nice and we're going to get whipped by the tail end of a storm, cyclone or hurricane flashing past.

The road twists and turns, getting gradually higher towards the Newlands Pass. It's a single-track road, but thankfully there is very little traffic. We reach the summit and then the road winds down towards Buttermere. I talk to Brendan constantly and am very aware of the gradients and the sharp bends. The road takes us into the centre of Buttermere. Again there are cars everywhere, filling every available space at the roadside. But this time it won't matter, as we have our own parking space at the hotel.

Buttermere, although generally referred to as a village, really isn't. It's a hamlet, though it has two hotels with public bars and two cafes, which is a lot for somewhere so small. There is no shop, not even a village store, and hardly any houses. There's no village centre as such, no green or focal point. The two hotels, as much as anything, mark the heart of the isolated little community.

There are a lot of people about as we drive slowly towards the Buttermere Court Hotel, which has views of the lake and is in a prime location. The car park has coned off spaces for residents. We're residents, so we gratefully occupy one of those spaces.

It takes me a while to realise that this is the former Fish Inn, an attractive whitewashed stone building. I've been in the Fish Inn, many years ago when on holiday with Nicky. We had visited Buttermere for the day and were walking along the adjacent trackway towards the lake, when we encountered an old lady who had fallen and it seemed likely she'd broken her ankle. Nicky stayed with her while I ran in to the Fish Inn to get help.

It was long before mobile phones – not that a mobile would have helped, as there is virtually no signal for miles. Inside, the Fish Inn was old fashioned – but not really in a good way; it was dated and tired. An older woman appeared. I say older, she was probably about 40 – I'd now call her a younger woman. I explained about the old lady and asked her to call an ambulance. She actually refused! She said she was too busy, that it wasn't her problem and, besides, an ambulance would take hours to arrive, so there was no point. I don't remember the exact conversation, but I was furious – and before I left the Fish Inn, the woman had indeed phoned for an ambulance.

We waited with the old lady until it arrived, which wasn't

too long at all, possibly up to half an hour and she was taken away. It put me off the Fish Inn and it tainted Buttermere.

The inn was eventually sold, revamped, rebranded and has emerged from its cocoon as the Buttermere Court Hotel. I leave Brendan in the van and head inside to book in. I wouldn't recognise it as the dusty old Fish Inn. It has a tasteful, classy period interior, comfortable and clean. I head towards the high reception desk and tell them my name. The lovely receptionist taps on the keyboard of the computer and then leans over the counter.

"And where's Brendan?"

I love that attention to detail. They know my dog's name!

"He's a bit busy at the moment."

We do a bit of dog chat. It turns out to be a very dog-friendly hotel. Brendan can even accompany me to breakfast, which was something that had concerned me.

"We all love dogs." she says. "We've all got dogs, all the staff. We love them."

That's so nice to hear. If only Brendan liked people, we'd all get on fine.

We're too early for our room, so I go and collect my boy from the van. I open the side door and he stretches and jumps out a little stiffly. I then realise he's been sick in his basket and there, pooled in the bottom of it is his breakfast. I suspect he was only sick at the last winding section, or even when I was in the hotel. Poor boy. I don't know what to do with the dirty towels so I shake them as best I can and then roll them up and put them in the storage area at the back of the van.

We set off towards the lake, through a muddy farm yard and then along a well-worn path which winds towards Buttermere. The path is fenced, so I let Brendan off his lead. He's meandering along quite happily. Being sick probably did him the world of good. He's tootling ahead of me. Two elderly men are coming through a gate towards us. I say urgently to Brendan: "Wait there!" Both men immediately stop. The first man looks at me quizzically. "What, me?"

I laugh. "If only my dog listened and obeyed like that!"

They both laugh, but still remain frozen on the spot. Seriously, if I had this power over Brendan life would be so much easier. I cancel the inertia spell and release the two chaps. Brendan allows them to pass, so all is well.

We drop down to Buttermere and stand on the shingle shore. At a mile and a half long, it is one of the smaller lakes. It is an oasis of beauty surrounded by high fells; there are startling views in every direction. I watch Brendan frolicking and exploring, sniffing and weeing. He's weed on more than three trees now, so according to dog law he owns Buttermere.

There are lots of lovely dogs and lots of dog people. Everyone is very friendly. People are saying things like "Afternoon." "Hello, lovely day." "What a handsome dog!" Brendan is only really interested in the third type of comment, until I remind him that he's supposedly very proudly British now, so he needs to embrace weather-talk wholeheartedly.

We continue along a well-trodden path above the lake, leading through a beautiful oak woodland. I've decided we're going to walk round the lake. Brendan has decided we aren't. He suddenly runs up a mossy bank and promptly sits down. A family group are approaching. They stop, smile and point at him.

"Oh, look at the dog!"

Brendan seems to be ignoring them and is staring resolutely across the lake.

"He's doing what we'd do…" an old man says. "…sitting and admiring the scenery."

I laugh. "He seems to admire the scenery an awful lot."

They move on, turning occasionally to look back at him. Brendan remains staring out over the water, as though they don't exist. I climb the mossy bank and sit down next to him in the spongy, dark green carpet with dappled light showing through the stirring canopy of leaves. A tiddling stream runs alongside us; I don't know if streams usually tiddle, but this one definitely does. It's another of those precious moments that will surely become a memory.

Nearby, a farm dog keeps barking. Brendan tilts his head, straining to hear what it's saying. Brendan learned English mainly from daytime TV; I'm not sure he can get to grips with the Cumbrian dialect, so he's struggling to comprehend what the dog is trying to communicate;

eventually he stops trying. He's so happy to be here, to be out in the fresh air, to be sitting down. He even picks up a twig and starts playfully chewing it, which he seldom does.

We set off again, and after a series of sit-downs, we eventually arrive at the shore, half way along the lake. Brendan has a paddle and a drink and lies down. I gaze at the view. Buttermere is absolutely stunning, surrounded by trees and basking in the sunshine. I'm so glad we came here.

Two ladies, possibly a mother and daughter, come and sit on a bench nearby. They slide off their rucksacks and begin eating something. Within minutes all the dogs in the area have flocked to them and are begging for food. It's like a scene from a film; hundreds of dogs have suddenly emerged from the trees, all shapes and sizes. I confess, when I say "hundreds", I mean closer to three, possibly four. Hot on their tails are people with leads, trying to snare the appropriate dog and guide them away, not very successfully. It's hilarious.

Not being food-motivated, Brendan has no interest in them at all and sits aloof and disapproving. I chuckle at the spectacle, but I laugh too soon, because Brendan is suddenly making a beeline for the bench and the ladies. He's obviously gone over to police the situation. The poor ladies are holding their bacon rolls aloft and trying to shoo the circling dogs away. I sprint through the trees towards the bench. As I approach there is a sudden horrified shrieking. Brendan has cocked his leg and is weeing on the older lady's rucksack, which is leaning against the bench. I stop him, clip him on his lead and pull him away, apologising profusely.

"I'm so sorry! He *never* does that! I don't know what came over him!" I'm absolutely mortified. "I'm *so* sorry!"

The woman is just staring at her rucksack. She hasn't said a word, which always makes a situation even worse.

"I think it was because of all the other dogs… I think he was claiming you as his own. You should really be flattered."

She isn't flattered. Neither would I be.

"I've got some water. Shall I rinse it off?" I get out my water bottle and carefully pour it over the affected area, washing away – or at least diluting – the urine. She seems satisfied with this and resumes eating her bacon roll, while we slink away between the oak boughs.

The footpath goes through a narrow tunnel cut through a rocky outcrop. It's quite long and quite dark and – it turns out – quite muddy. We wait for a couple to come through. The man steps into the light, turns round to look for his wife, sees she's some distance behind in the darkness, sighs, rolls his eyes and walks off muttering. The woman eventually appears, stepping very carefully.

"Thanks for waiting." she says. "I didn't want to get my new boots muddy."

That's going to happen one day. Probably very soon. It comes to all of us. Except to me, as my boots are in the back of the car – at home. I forgot them, so I'm walking along in trainers – the cardinal sin.

By four o'clock the sun is dipping below the peaks on the other side of the lake. It's getting cooler and the colour is fading, so we head back towards the village and the hotel. We meet a nice couple with their young daughter and a very active labradoodle.

"Did you walk all the way round the lake?" the man asks.

"No, I intended to," I nod towards Brendan. "…but he had a different idea."

They look at Brendan, who's using the opportunity to have a sit down whilst ignoring the other dog.

The man is frowning. "Oh… Is he old?"

"He's ten, but he's always been like this. He's bone idle."

"Oh god," the woman says wearily, "I wish ours was like that. He's never tired…" Her voice is rising in pitch. "He never stops… He *never* stops. If we don't walk all the way round the lake, we won't get any peace. He'll drive us mad. Mad!"

I can't help thinking that judging by the manic edge to her voice it might already be too late.

The man is still frowning. "I can't believe a dog doesn't love walking and running… Ours just can't get enough."

"That's because yours is a real dog."

The woman says suddenly – and a bit desperately. "I'll swap you! Seriously! I could handle that. That's my kind of dog. We could swap!"

Brendan stands up, because he thinks she means it – and I think she means it. He isn't up for a dog-swap. Probably because he has very exacting standards and it would take too long to train a new set of humans. We bid them farewell – quite hastily – and each carry on, in opposite directions, with the dog we started out with.

It's funny, but I've interacted with more people today than I did on the whole of the rest of the trip. Everyone has said hello and chatted. Not one person has just stared in horror and said nothing. It's been really refreshing.

We had lots of sit-downs on the way out, so this means we have to sit down at all the same places on the way back. It's one of Brendan's "things". So, we duly sit down, but only very briefly at each location. The closer we get to the hotel, the faster Brendan goes. It looks like he's eager to check into his room.

When we get back it is nearly dark and the hotel is like a shining beacon. The inn has lake views, though our room doesn't; we have a view over the back door of the kitchens. The room, however, is really nice. A twin room, very comfortable, very clean and with a gigantic wall-mounted television, which Brendan loves. He'll be flicking through the TV channels all night.

We head down to the bar for tea. It's very nice, only moderately busy. Brendan is ready for a long rest, so he stretches out and goes to sleep with immediate effect. I'm trying to veer towards healthier food, after my – as yet still undiagnosed – suspect gall bladder or pancreas or something else attack in Windermere. I order a falafel salad bowl, which is lovely, along with a strange and fruity alcohol-free lager, which is quite odd, but also quite compelling.

We have a short walk afterwards around the village in the dark. It's very quiet; we see no one, though the bars of both hotels are warmly lit and filled with people. There is no light in the village. There are no lampposts or anything; it's pitch black. The clouds are low and there is no moon; there are no stars. After a circuit of the village and an intense sniff, Brendan pulls me back to the hotel, runs up the stairs to our room and leaps onto his bed.

I have just read a sign downstairs, saying that the Fish Inn, as this building used to be, was the home of the Maid of Buttermere. I know this as a book by Melvin Bragg, from my days working in the bookshop; this was a bestseller at the time. It turns out the book was based on a real person, the attractive daughter of the inn keeper of the Fish Inn. She was tricked into marrying a man who turned out to be a right wrong-un: a bigamist and forger. He was eventually found out and hanged for his various crimes.

We have a relaxing evening, enjoying the warmth and comfort of our hotel room. Brendan relaxes more than I do, but then he practices a lot. A *lot.*

We keep hearing warnings about the approaching storm, which is an "intense extratropical cyclone". Apparently. It's causing devastation around Europe and was due to make itself known here towards the end of the week, but today's news warns that it's put its foot down and will be arriving ahead of schedule. In fact, it's imminent. We should be affected by it from tomorrow.

* * * * * * * * * *

Brendan didn't wake me up for his night feed, probably because he was too tired. This is quite unusual. His pancreatic condition is much worse at night and he needs regular small meals to keep it in line. Possibly as a result of him missing his night feed, he now won't eat anything. It's not just a case of him refusing to eat, he seems to be actively afraid of any food I put down for him and runs away from it, regardless of what it is. I try not to let this worry me and hope he will come round later.

But it does worry me, because without food to keep everything lubricated and running smoothly, it will get worse and he'll have a major flare-up. But I can't do anything about that, and me getting stressed about it won't help; Brendan will pick up on my stress and he'll get stressed, then I'll get more stressed. It's a vicious circle. And regardless of how I try, I am getting increasingly stressed.

We go for breakfast in the plush drawing room, which is set aside for those with dogs. There is only one other table occupied this morning, by a family and small dog that looks like hand luggage. I have a nice breakfast, tomatoes, mushrooms, beans, wilted spinach, smashed avocado and toast. Brendan stretches out under the table, enjoying the thick carpet; he especially enjoys the tasteful and slightly regal pattern, as we only have plain soft furnishings at home. We're both enjoying this experience far more than having breakfast in the van.

I try Brendan with food again, but he adamantly refuses, so we head out, walking from the hotel to Crummock Water. It was supposed to be a nice, sunny day, but it isn't. It's actually quite dull and grey, cool and breezy and the clouds are low, but we're in the Lake District, we're at Buttermere, surrounded by fells and lakes and streams, so we're feeling very lucky.

Brendan seems quite happy as he trundles along the winding pathway. We encounter several other dogs. Brendan is desperate to get to them and whenever he does, he sits down and haughtily ignores them. He's loving it.

The path eventually brings us to Crummock Water, stretching out before us. Considering Crummock Water and Buttermere are so close and were once the same lake, they have very different atmospheres. Buttermere is soft and green, Crummock is much more dramatic, rugged, surrounded by more imposing fells and more rock. Along the shoreline there is marram grass, marshes and bracken. It is still an attractive lake in its own right, but much less chocolate-box than its neighbour.

I suggest to Brendan that we walk to Loweswater village and have lunch at the pub there. Brendan suggests we don't. We get about a quarter of the way and even after many, many sit downs it becomes obvious that Brendan isn't going to get that far – mainly because he's made his mind up. He decides we need to turn round and go back. We're paying a lot for a nice hotel room in a beautiful location – which has a huge flatscreen TV – and yet we're wasting time coming out for a walk, which we can do any day of the week. He can't rationalise it. We set off back to the village and the hotel.

After a few more minutes, he decides heading back is just as tiring as heading forwards; he plonks himself down on the grass. I carry on walking and call him. I carry on walking and beckon energetically to him. I carry on walking and call him again. He is staring at me intently, but not making a move. Again, I think I can't give in. I carry on walking. He's still staring, sitting upright, a short distance off the path. He now looks very small and very far away.

An old couple are coming towards me. I say hello. "Can you tell my dog to get a move on, please."

"Oh, there's no point me saying anything." The woman says, "Dogs don't listen to me!"

"They clearly don't listen to me either!" I say.

The man just smiles and moves silently past.

I watch as they draw nearer to Brendan. I didn't really expect them to go up to him, but the man has stepped off the path towards him. My heart starts racing. I start walking rapidly towards them thinking: *"Please don't go any closer!"*

The man stops a safe distance away. Brendan is still sitting, so presumably doesn't feel threatened. I can tell the man is talking to him, pointing back towards me. It doesn't look as though Brendan is answering. Then the man gives up and the couple continue on their way. When I get up to him, I put Brendan on his lead and he won't be coming off again. (Until next time I let him off.)

In the afternoon, I insist we head out to the little church to see the Wainright memorial. True to form, Brendan insists we don't. We have a few words and I win. We step out of the hotel and are nearly knocked over by a gale force wind. It screeches and there is rattling all around, doors, windows, gates. It's very dramatic. It's gone cloudy, grey and ominous. It feels like the storm might be upon us. We dash up the steps to the little church and force the heavy door shut behind us, against the maelstrom.

The church is a simple stone building; I'd call it a chapel really. I'm not sure about the protocols of going in with Brendan. There is no one in, so we advance along the aisle, at which point an older lady appears from a curtained doorway. She smiles, says hello and bids us to come fully in. She has a thick mane of curly hair and looks quite Bohemian, but she's wearing wellies and a body-warmer rather than a kaftan.

"Make yourselves at home! Don't mind me."

We chat about the weather – we're British, it's what we do. Regardless of what he might say, Brendan isn't British and at present he just can't be bothered to feign interest in the subject, so he sits down instead and yawns a lot.

"It's so windy!" the woman exclaims.

"It is!"

"It's just come out of nowhere!"

"It has!"

"The last time we had weather like this, next door's trampoline blew over the roof of our house. I just saw something fly past the window and there it was... gone. I live in Loweswater. We do get the wind in Loweswater."

She disappears off behind her curtain and leaves us alone in the church. The Wainwright memorial is a commemorative slate plaque in a window, out of which there is a view over Buttermere to Wainwright's favourite fell, Haystacks, with its distinctive fist-like summit.

PAUSE AND REMEMBER

ALFRED WAINWRIGHT

LIFT UP YOUR EYES TO HAYSTACKS

HIS FAVOURITE PLACE

1907 – 1991.

Wainwright was a Lancashire accountant who enjoyed walking the fells on his days off, as a way to escape the bustle of town life and enjoy the countryside. He rose to worldwide fame when his handwritten and hand-drawn guidebooks to the Lakeland fells became popular, years after they were written. They were a labour of love for Wainwright and the massive and enduring success was quite irrelevant to him. When I was working in Waterstones in my youth, his books were being reformatted into photographic, coffee-table volumes and were bestsellers. He became an iconic figure and TV celebrity and like an adopted father to the Lakes.

In his autobiographical work, *Fellwanderer*, he wrote poignantly: "Every day that passes is a day less. That day will come when there is nothing left but memories."

He died in 1991 of a heart attack, aged 84. Years before he had made it known that he wanted his ashes scattered on his favourite fell, Haystacks, close to Innominate Tarn – the tarn with no name.

"I shall go to it, for the last time, and be carried…"

His second wife Betty walked up with his ashes and scattered them as requested.

"And if you, dear reader, should get a bit of grit in your boot as you are crossing Haystacks in the years to come, please treat it with respect. It might be me."

* * * * * * * * * *

After the church, we run across the village to one of the two cafes. I order a black americano and two vegan Bakewell tarts.

"Ah, is one for your dog?" the friendly girl on the till asks.

"Nope." I say. "They're both for me."

We sit upstairs in the haybarn-like loft. The Bakewells are gorgeous and the coffee is the best I have had in a long time. I'm having a lovely feast and Brendan is having a nap, so we're both happy for the moment.

Afterwards, we walk to the lake again. Buttermere is like a raging ocean, with waves rolling to the shore, whereas yesterday there were gentle ripples and none of this violence. We sit on the shingle for some time just watching the waves, until the weak sun is sinking behind the high fells and it's getting colder and even windier. We wander off along the shore, in the general direction of the hotel.

Brendan is scouring the water's edge, nose to the ground, looking for something very important. He won't reveal what it is he's looking for, but he's determined he won't give up until he's found it. Then suddenly he gives up – having not found it – and walks off.

Since yesterday, a gregarious collie has wrestled ownership of Buttermere from Brendan, so he has to urgently race around weeing on every available tree, rock, gatepost or tuft of grass, until he's sure his scent has overwritten all others and ownership is back with him.

We get back to our hotel and I again try Brendan with small amounts of all his various high-quality, luxurious and expensive foods, but he still refuses to eat. It's making me really stressed, which doesn't help. His stomach is growling. He hasn't eaten all day; he has acid reflux or pancreatitis, so not eating really isn't good for him. I give him one of his tablets, but there is no apparent improvement. I decide a change of scenery might have a positive effect, so we go down to the bar. One lager later and he's still no different. He is clearly in some degree of discomfort.

We head out for a late-night wee walk. There is no one on the reception desk, which is quite odd. Out in the darkness it's so blustery; I love it. The air is bristling with the power of the wind; it's almost electric. I love the elements; Brendan prefers soft furnishings.

The village is completely deserted. The hotel bars are closed, the lights are off, so there is no warmth. It's very dark. Tonight, the clouds have cleared and we can see the stars covering the dome of the sky.

When we go back inside reception is still unmanned. We meet no one in the hotel corridors and hear no sounds from the closed doors that we walk past. It's quite eerie. Perhaps they have all been evacuated because of the storm and we've been left behind.

Brendan is still refusing food. Every time I offer him some new tempting morsel he seems to be getting increasingly panicky.

Nicky texts to warn that the worst of the storm is now coming tomorrow and there have been all manner of warnings about threat to life. What we're experiencing now is like the pre-storm, just sent ahead to soften us up, but nothing compared to the onslaught that's approaching.

Brendan lies beside me, dozing fitfully, his stomach grinding like an out of tune orchestra; it's deafening. It's an awful evening and the drama of the weather outside is wasted on us.

I'm very worried about him and feel so sorry for him. I think he's in discomfort rather than pain, but it's awful to see. Sometimes he looks at me, as though expecting me to make it stop, but I've done all I can do and it's just a waiting game – eventually it will pass.

I feel so down. I can't focus on the television, I can't read.

I just end up stroking him and staring at him. I thought this would be such a treat and such a great way to end our trip in style, but I just wish we were at home.

I realise I've forgotten to have any food, as I've been too concerned about Brendan. My van is parked outside, so I can actually go out and cook anything I want, but I can't be bothered and it's too late. I have a wedge of dry malt loaf instead and try to watch an episode of *The Persuaders* which I find on one of the hundreds of channels.

After his second tablet, Brendan seems more relaxed. His growling stomach eases off and he sleeps quite soundly and peacefully.

At 7.17am the first person of the day walks past our door and Brendan resumes his barking duties, which I take as a good sign.

We've had our two nights in the hotel and now we're really heading home. Brendan being ill has ruined everything. I'm now more convinced than ever that we need to get rid of the van and never come on holiday again.

Brendan seems perky enough when we go out for our pre-breakfast walk. The trees are thrashing, the grass seems like it's almost being torn up by the roots, the air is grey and grainy. The surrounding fells look dark and oppressive. We walk past the campsite. There are a few tents still remaining; some brave souls are apparently planning to ride out the storm.

After breakfast – mushrooms and tomatoes on toast – we

walk to the head of Buttermere. Brendan scampers along quite happily; it looks like the attack is fully over and he is back to his normal self. His tail is aloft and his ears are being blown back, making him look permanently startled – and perhaps he is.

The water is wild, as though it's boiling. I love extremes of weather like this; I could stay here all day. Unfortunately, Brendan has had a tranquiliser – it is prescribed; he isn't an addict – and he needs to get back to his basket soon.

I'm sorry to leave Buttermere, especially because of the intense weather. Back at the van, Brendan instals himself gratefully in his basket and we set off. I'm a bit sad driving away, because this doesn't just feel like the end of our trip, it seems like the end of holidays for us.

Brendan is relaxed and drowsy, but not properly asleep. On the winding parts – of which there are many – I talk to him constantly. Often it is a running commentary on the scenery. "There are a lot of dark clouds over in the west. Look at those trees… beautiful. The drystone walls are so well-built, aren't they?" Brendan couldn't be less interested if he tried. And believe me, he tried. "That's a nice cottage… You'd love that wouldn't you… because of the garden." But he wouldn't like it – because it's not home.

The van isn't smelling very good today. It smells rotten, pungent, rank. I'm not sure what it can be, but it's like something has died in it. I open the window, thinking it will blow the stench away, but it seems to be getting worse. Then I remember there are two vomit-covered towels in the back that I'd completely forgotten about. They've been quietly festering for 48 hours. It's disgusting.

I'm glad when we're finally done with the tightly winding lanes and we join a dual carriageway and then the M6, and we're travelling smoothly and Brendan can go to sleep properly.

It's all going well until we get near Manchester, when all the red tail-lights come on and the traffic is at a standstill. There hasn't been an accident or anything; this is normal. Welcome home.

* * * * * * * * *

If Brendan Was A Human...

Human Brendan is quite eccentric. He doesn't feel he has to conform. He doesn't mind being considered odd. He doesn't *need* to fit in; he doesn't *want* to fit in, which is just as well, because he couldn't fit in if he tried.

ABOVE: Our hotel, nestling beneath the high fells.

ABOVE: Brendan has a nice sit down in the oak woodland above Buttermere.

ABOVE: Buttermere

ABOVE: Buttermere – which has now become one of my favourite lakes.

EPILOGUE

I think, all things considered, we had a remarkable trip. I have many treasured memories of lovely times spent with my boy, such as the first evening when we went for a walk along the shore of Windermere. It seemed like we were at the beginning of a great adventure and we had it all to look forward to, but 24 hours later I had been on to the emergency doctor and we were hurtling down the motorway heading home.

Since completing the trip, I had a blood screening and an ultrasound, which revealed that I have a minor issue with my liver. It can't be controlled by medication or any procedure, it has to be dealt with by diet and lifestyle, so – like Brendan – I'm on a very healthy, very low-fat diet and a sharp increase in exercise. This basically means a severe reduction of cake, which I don't like, but needs must.

We now have His and His separate walks; a leisurely stroll to the field for Brendan and a speed-walk or run for me. Though I have to say, Brendan is so much more active than he was before the trip: some days he actually runs all the way to the field, because he's so excited and energised.

I have read that the best thing for dogs with aging and stiff limbs is to increase walking on a gradient. The undulating nature of the Lake District has definitely had a hugely beneficial effect on Brendan. We live in a very flat area; our nearest hill is ten miles away, so our regular walks are all on the level; although it won't be easy, we need to do our best to have a hill walk whenever we can.

Several people have commented on how puppy-like Brendan now appears to be. On a few occasions he's caused considerable consternation by "running around" or "chasing another dog" or "playing" or "being awake". Don't worry, in-between these moments of activity, he's still no stranger to his usual hobbies of standing still, staring into space, sitting down, lying down and sleeping in a public area.

I was determined to bring back something positive from the Lakes and incorporate it into my homelife. One day, when we were walking to the field, I decided I would say hello to the very next person we passed. It turned out to be an elderly man. I issued him with a friendly smile and a jaunty "Hello". He paused and looked traumatised; there was a long hesitation, then he said hello back and he seemed genuinely and pleasantly surprised. There is a chance that he initially thought the greeting was a prelude to mugging him and then when I didn't actually mug him, he was ecstatic. Perhaps he went on to say hello to someone else, perhaps I created a Mexican wave of greetings. Or perhaps it stopped there, a solitary hello between strangers. Whatever the case, I did my bit.

The Lake District was stunningly beautiful, and now that we're home, we just want to go back again. Well, I want to go back again; Brendan doesn't. When the sun shines, I often find myself thinking "I wonder what it's like in the Lakes right now." I already know what it's like: it's amazing.

We visited all sixteen lakes; we called at many places I'd been to before and knew well; it was a sometimes pleasing and sometimes poignant trip down Memory Lane. Hopefully I've made a lot of new memories with my boy. We spent a lot of time just sitting beside lakes in the sunshine, enjoying the moment and those were the very best times of all.

* * * * * * * * * *

If Brendan Was A Human...

He'd be me.

EXTRAS

The Quirks Of Brendan Freedog

10 Facts That Make Living With Brendan Very...erm... *Interesting.*

1. He's frightened of water and never drinks.
2. He hates silver bowls.
3. He hates slow moving vehicles.
4. He is SO fussy about his food. What he likes today he won't like tomorrow. He isn't food motivated, so cannot be bribed with treats.
5. He barks at planes.
6. He is very lazy. He usually enjoys going out for his morning walk, but quite actively dislikes all subsequent walks.
7. He dislikes dogs that are larger than he is and will bark and growl at them, whilst he is quite wary around small dogs.
8. He dislikes any form of motorised travel.
9. He loves eavesdropping.
10. He will not play with a ball or fetch a stick.

ABOVE: Laughing Boy. He's My Boy and he's laughing. Not sure what at; I'm probably better off not knowing.

A Very Useful Guide To Cumbrian Dialect

Some useful words - though probably not all that useful.

FELL: Hill or mountain

TARN: Pond, small lake

BECK: Stream

YAN: One

TAN: Two

TETHERER: Three

JEWKLE: Dog

YATTER: Talk

YAM: Home (One of Brendan's favourite words)

CHUNTER: Mutter incoherently

NETTY: Toilet

Some Everyday Useful Phrases

HOYING IT DOON! Raining heavily (A very useful phrase)

HASTS IVER DEEKED A CUDDY LOUP A FIVE BAR YAT? Have you ever seen a donkey jump a five-bar gate? (Probably less useful, but good to know)

ARS GARN YAM. I'm going home (One of Brendan's favourite phrases)

EXCUSE ME BUT YOUR DOG'S IN MY LIVING ROOM CHANGING CHANNELS TO CASH IN THE ATTIC, EATING MY HOBNOBS AND CRITICISING MY WALLPAPER. This is actually the same in most dialects.

The Past Is A Foreign County: My Lakeland – In Old Photos

Photography has changed such a lot over the years. My first camera was a "happy snapper" – you point, you press – and you had no control over any aspect of the photograph. You had to wait ages until the roll of film was completed, then you had to have it developed. At one time this generally meant sending it away, later taking it to a high street photo shop. Usually, the photos you got back were months, sometimes years old. They were so expensive you didn't take endless pictures of something, as you might today. Each photo was precious. And very often absolutely rubbish.

ABOVE: Inside looking out: Rydal cave. This is one of my earliest surviving photographs of my Lakes visits. It was from a Youth Hostelling trip, possibly with school, or possibly soon after with friends.

ABOVE: Our family dog, Gemma, trying out Mum and Dad's first camper van, a blue classic VW with elevating roof. It was very basic and quite old fashioned inside, but it was great. I accompanied them to the Lake District. I assume I stayed in my tent with Gemma, but I don't actually remember.

ABOVE: Mum and Dad at the Castlerigg stone circle. I must have taken them there, because they wouldn't have gone otherwise. They must have thought "Oh... some stones in a field." I'm guessing this must have been around 1980 – otherwise a warrant would have been issued for the arrest of my father and his shorts. Notice there is no one else at the stone circle. You wouldn't get that now.

ABOVE: Nicky with Cindy at Wray Castle on the western shore of Windermere. Our B&B, the Dower House, was in the grounds of the castle. For our very first holiday together we had no car and walked here from the station at Windermere. It was MILES! It's a stunning location, a short stroll to the lake, but quite a long walk to anywhere else, such as a pub or cafe.This was our only holiday without Cindy, who stayed with Nicky's mum. It wasn't right without her. For the second trip we had a car and Cindy came with us.

We came to the Lakes a lot. We loved it. It was a special place for the three of us. We looked into moving to Lakeland at one point and began researching jobs, but it never came to anything. Our lives would have been completely different. I'm not saying better or worse, but very different.

ABOVE: Camping near Elterwater. Cindy peering out of my tent. Nicky was probably inside trying to find the plug for her hair dryer. There were so many complaints from both of them about the camping experience, and yet they consented to go again – several times.

ABOVE: Nicky on Todd Crag, with Windermere in the background. It's quite an easy walk and you're rewarding with the brilliant view, covering the whole of the northern part of the lake. We did this walk a lot. It's a real shame that Brendan refused to do it. I think he could easily have made it once he got going, though we wouldn't have been able to park anywhere in the area so it's all irrelevant.

ABOVE: Brendan's Uncle Steve with Jake. We were camping at Consiton Hall campsite. Here we are climbing the Coniston Old Man, which has been cited as the most climbed Lakeland fell. It's a great walk. This photograph sends shudders down Brendan's spine; he has always maintained that if dogs walk too high they explode. Jake here disproves Brendan's rather feeble and transparent theory.

ABOVE: Wastwater looking quite verdant. I think I was with Steve again and we were camping in the next valley, Eskdale and had walked over the tops. In those days, before Brendan, walks were generally further than car park to café. I can't actually believe the dramatic Wasdale valley looks so lush and green! It looks beautiful.

ABOVE: Jake with my schoolfriend, Paul. Notice how he's holding on to Jake – he wouldn't attempt this with Brendan. Paul prefers to communicate with Brendan via email – preferably from another country.

ABOVE: My boy, Jake. When Jake died I decided I would never have another dog: they become such a large part of your life. Hopefully, you get to spend many, many years with them, but in a way that just makes it even harder to be without them. Despite my vow, after twenty dog-free years I then met Brendan Freedog. He used a mixture of hypnotism and psychotropic drugs to recondition me and make me foster him. The rest is history. Our history.

A Note From The Authors

Thank you for buying our book and thank you for reading it; we are truly grateful and hope you have enjoyed it! Please consider putting a review on Amazon – it really makes a difference. Until next time, take care.

Gray & Brendan

https://www.facebook.com/BrendanFreedog

ALSO FROM GRAY FREEMAN

underdogs:
How a man and a street dog form an unbreakable
bond and a lifechanging friendship.

This is a book about a friendship between two people – except one of them is a dog. Together they were more than the sum of their parts. They embarked upon a journey of discovery around Britain: a life-changing tour which would ensure that they either stayed together forever... or never spoke again.

Underdogs is funny, light-hearted, sometimes poignant, often heart-warming. It is about a journey and about over-coming adversity.

It is about the challenges of adopting a damaged soul and the joys of spending every day with your best friend. Brendan crept into Gray's life when he most needed him, changed it around to suit himself and then had a nap.

DOG DAYS:
underdogs II

Finding they were unable to return to a life on the road as the coronavirus cast its black shadow over the world, Gray and Brendan decided to use the time to try and improve themselves, and – most importantly – to try and find positivity in every day. This began well, but it wasn't long before their world started to fall apart.

Dog Days is a diary of that unprecedented period in history. It is in turns touching, funny, optimistic, poignant, tragic and very human. Despite everything going wrong in the world, *Dog Days* is about the joy of spending every second of every day with your best friend.

the underdog:
TRAVELS BEFORE BRENDAN
The Prequel to underdogs

Gray Freeman sets off in a van on a voyage of self-discovery - to fulfil a dream and travel around the coast of Britain. Without a dog! What was he thinking?

The plan was to see hidden corners of Britain and to explore remote coastlines, clifftops and forgotten byways, backwaters and other places that haven't yet been used to build shopping malls.

This was to be a life-changing experience, but not everything went according to plan.

The underdog is travel writing, but it is humorous and accessible, light-hearted and quirky. It is a celebration of travel, a love letter to the British coast.

This was to be the journey of a lifetime – and this is where it all began.

The Long Goodbye

And Other Plays

NOTHING IS AS IT SEEMS.

The Long Goodbye was a play. It was staged twice in Manchester. People laughed, people cried, people said how much they could relate to it. You will also be able to relate to it. It is funny, tragic and touching; it leaves a lasting impression.

YOU WAKE UP AND A WHOLE NEW LIFE HAS BEEN WRITTEN FOR YOU – A LIFE YOU KNOW MUST BE A LIE.

The Long Goodbye made a humorous, moving and memorable piece of theatre, and here it is presented as a "reading script" – between a script and a novel. It is accessible, at times laugh-out-loud funny and also deeply poignant. On the page it doesn't lose any of its humour or haunting impact.

EVERYTHING IS BIZARRE AND SURREAL, LIKE A 'SIXTIES TV SHOW. YOUR LIFE IS A PRISON; YOU ARE THE PRISONER.